KYLEE VAN DER VUURST

Walk With Me

Copyright

 Published by Kylee Van Der Vuurst with the assistance of Dragonfly Publishing Services, November 2024.

© All rights reserved by the author.

Apart from any fair dealing for the purpose of private study, research, criticism or review, as permitted under the Copyright Act, no part of this book may be reproduced by any process without written permission from the publisher.

The views expressed in this work are solely those of the author and do not necessarily reflect the views of the publishing services provider, and the publishing services provider hereby disclaims any responsibility for them.

 A catalogue record for this work is available from the National Library of Australia

ISBN (sc): 978-1-7635525-6-2
ISBN (e): 978-1-7635525-7-9

Copy edited by Zoë Hoffman
Printed in Australia

Dedication

Learning and growing takes unique opportunities to be challenged emotionally. For this reason, I want to thank all the people and situations which have challenged me to step up and become the person I needed to be to write this book.

To the people who made me question my worth and place in the world, without you, I wouldn't have been able to see and acknowledge my greatness.

Finally, to all the people who helped with the creation of this book. I am so grateful for your time and energy.

Contents

Introduction - Not Another Boring Personal Development Book   1

1 - The Cave	5
2 – It All Starts With a Wake-up Call	39
3 - Gratitude	43
4 - The Ego	52
5 - Listen to Understand	60
6 - Friends, Family, and the Lessons We Learn	64
7 - Intimate Relationships	73
8 - Letting Go of People with Love	80
9 - Be Unpopular	86
10 - Program Your Brain for Success	91
11 - Create a Vision	106
12 - Manifesting and Goals	116
13 - Setting and Achieving Your Goals	125
14 - Habits	131
15 - Turning Problems into Possibilities	137
16 - Is it Time to Take Control?	143
17 - Fear	150

18 - Your Triad of Self	155
19 - Always Be True to You	166
20 - The Gift of Vulnerability	175
21 - Self-Care	181
22 - Respect You	188
23 - You are Never Alone	195
24 - Signs From Above	202
25 - Stay in the Question	208
26 - Is Self-Judgement Stealing Your Peace?	213
27 - Failure to Launch	220
28 - Tomorrow is Uncertain	227
29 - Final Note	234

About

For Further Information

Introduction

Not Another Boring Personal Development Book

Throughout my personal development journey, I have come across books I have struggled to read. Sometimes, there was too much science, or the language just seemed boring. In writing this book, I wanted to write something easy to read. A book that you could laugh with, cry with and enjoy turning each page. Much of what I have included has come from my experiences and the awareness I have gained from teachers, books, relationships and watching the world around me. It is a gift to learn from the world around you and to embrace the times when that same world is challenging you.

The purpose of this book is to share the experiences and learnings which changed my life. If it reaches just one person and changes their life in an extraordinary way, then it's achieved its purpose.

Change comes to those who are ready. If it's your time, be courageous, bold and daring to venture into the dark places of your soul. The further you are willing to delve, the more you will transform in the process and become a positive example for those around you.

At the beginning of my journey, I was simply looking to escape the "Cave of Despair". It was dark, cold and unrelenting. I was white knuckled, with anxiety and depression my permanent state of mind. This was due to hating myself and what felt like a constant barrage of suffering and pain. I had accepted that this would be my life, a life without joy or possibility. I was dull and lifeless on the inside. My Cave was my suffering *and* my sanctuary for my teen and young adult life. It almost seems surreal I ever escaped.

Today, I am blessed. My internal world is flooded with vibrant colour. I'm lucky enough to have a heart filled with love and kindness I wish to radiate out into the world every single day. There is possibility around every corner, and every new challenge is an opportunity to grow and become an even greater version of myself. There are days I find myself climbing higher up the mountain of life as I continue to grow; other days are about surrendering and being in allowance of life.

There have been many challenges throughout my life. Now, with a greater understanding of myself and through determining my purpose, I see these challenges. My stubborn desire for a greater life has allowed me to experience it in a whole new way. That alone leaves me to wonder, *what else is possible?*

I share some heavy experiences in this book. My desire is for you to take the strength and courage from my story and lean into the possibility that something greater is also available to you.

What I find so interesting is how much of yourself you can find in another's story of growth and their courage to not be defined by their past. You discover opportunities for yourself. You can create a new space to strive for, which may have previously seemed out of reach.

Sometimes, in hearing another's story, you judge and compare your life to theirs. You may not have experienced the same extent of struggle and despair, so wonder what your excuse is. Always remember you are perfectly placed on your own personal journey. Other times, wounds are deep and wide. It's here you discover there are more options available to us than we may have realised. It's in these moments you find an invitation to choose something greater and learn that you don't have to be defined by your past.

I hope to have a positive impact on the world through my work while living a life full of love, kindness, fun and adventure. This becomes possible through what I choose to do and who I choose to be in this crazy world, every single day. I believe it is the legacy you leave that truly defines you and makes for a life worth living. This legacy can be built in our day-to-day interactions, not just in grand gestures or goals.

I promise to be raw, real and not sugar coat things. The world doesn't make hard truths easier to digest. The lion will still eat the zebra whether we like it or not. The world is unwavering, challenging and sometimes dark, but there is also so much joy, beauty, and love to be experienced. It all depends on where you choose to point your focus. It is important to acknowledge that the dark times unlock your growth and provide the opportunities to become all you can be.

If this book finds you whilst you are in your own Cave, lean on my courage and faith. And for those who are feeling the sun on your face, breathe in, embrace all the possibility. Take this moment to celebrate how far you have already come and the possibility of how far you can go.

To provide a deeper understanding about me and my life and how it has led me to writing this book, I thought there seemed no better place to start than at the beginning. So, let's begin.

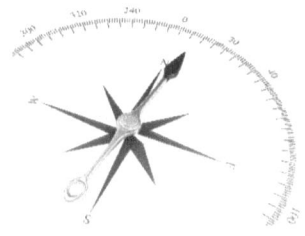

1 - The Cave

Life has provided many twists and turns. It has allowed me to learn and grow in many ways. Each experience has held a lesson to absorb and embody. I have been knocked down, teased, and had to fight for what was right. I have also had the opportunity to experience love, joy and hope.

There are so many reasons why I considered not including my story in the book or putting it at the back so it could easily be skimmed over. I had to check in with myself to ensure I was sharing for the right reasons. My story has shameful moments and things one might like to hide, yet this is precisely why I want to share. So often, you feel ashamed of the circumstances and situations in your life that challenged you most. Whether it's bad decision-making or things that happened to you. I have a nice collection of both.

It's time to change the narrative. Instead of looking at the circumstances of your life through the lens of shame, it's time to embrace your stories with the acknowledgement that they are the foundation from which you grow and learn.

The foundation is the most important part of creating any quality product. It is the prep work to a paint job or the structural foundation of a home. This framework is important for the end result to be exactly what it was intended to be, to meet the master plan. I believe each of us is here for a reason. Nothing in life is by accident, therefore your foundation is no accident. You have been through precisely what was required for you to learn what you are here to learn, to become the person you are meant to be.

The Cave, for me, was comfortable, familiar, yet soul-destroying. The Cave was the place I allowed myself to be a victim. I was not in control of my life, depressed to the point of being suicidal, anxious and self-hating, and I hid this world away from everyone. It was a secret place. For a long time, no one was allowed in, because then they would know the truth—that I was not happy at all. I had a wonderful mask, which I always wore. It told the outside world that I was happy and loving life, but I was a mess on the inside. Sexual abuse, family violence, promiscuity, feeling unlovable, drugs, alcohol, bad choices, and so much more had pushed me into The Cave, and it kept me feeling unworthy and unlovable for years.

When you're younger, you don't understand how your experiences can shape your life. During those first seven years of life, you're a sponge, absorbing everything. Watching and learning from your parents for how to act in different situations. You learn when you're safe and what things to be fearful of. You learn when it's okay to speak and when to simply keep your mouth shut. You learn everything from soaking up the world around you.

The life behind closed doors…

I grew up in an idyllic part of the world. Beautiful forest, a river and small waterfall on my doorstep. There was always something to do or explore. Swimming in summer, exploring the wild river during winter, and enjoying the abundance of wildflowers during spring. My parents were hard-working, positive members of the community. Both were involved in local sporting groups. Mum was a nurse and Dad a carpenter. My older brother and I were typical siblings, arguing when we weren't getting along. Yet this magical, normal life hid secrets from the outside world.

My dad was incredibly aggressive towards my older brother and Mum. He also drank heavily. Violence came out of nowhere. I recall one evening when Mum, Dad, my brother and I were sitting around the kitchen table having dinner when Dad snapped. My gaze turned to my lap, and I tried to be invisible. This night, what set Dad off was the way my brother was eating his food. From what I had seen, he wasn't doing anything out of the ordinary, but I dared not say a word. My brother was sent to his room, and Dad followed him shortly after. Now, my dad wasn't a small guy. He was over six feet tall and strong. Mum soon followed Dad, and the yelling began, leaving me at the empty table with full plates.

After a while, I also headed towards my brother's room. The yelling was well and truly underway. I walked around the corner to where my room shared a small corridor with my brother's. I stood in the doorway to my brother's room. I saw him on the floor, getting kicked by my dad, while Mum tried to stop him. I must have made a noise, because I was pushed across the corridor into my room, and my brother's door was slammed shut. The cries, pleas from my mum, and the yelling continued behind the closed door as I sat on the floor of my room alone, sobbing to myself. After this incident, my brother, Mum and I ended up at the house of Mum's friend. My brother was pretty beaten up. Yet, we always returned. In this instance it was much later that evening.

Another time, I was helping Mum in the kitchen with the dishes when Dad came in. He yelled at Mum that I shouldn't have to do the dishes. My dad then walked out onto the veranda and threw the outdoor table over the edge—there was quite a large drop-off due to the fall of the land towards the river. Dad came back in, and the argument continued. It ended up with Dad pulling Mum's hair as she called my omah—Dad's mum—to tell her what her son was up to. Mum talking through her tears, Dad yelling. This led to more yelling and eventually, they realised I was there, and I was told to get to my room. I diligently obeyed.

No one believed Mum when she tried to tell them what was happening, not even her parents. The doctors Mum spoke to about his behaviour change didn't even believe her either; they knew the sociable man they drank and played sport with. We were alone in our beautiful hell. Except for mum's closest friend and confidant.

Growing up in this chaotic world, we never knew when Dad would lose his cool next. Mum had developed a sign for us kids to get out of the house and into the car quickly and lock the doors. The sign was to rub her finger under her nose.

Eventually, Mum left Dad, and we moved into a rental next door to my friend's house. We found a sense of peace. Unfortunately, the peace didn't last. My brother and I begged Mum not to go back, but she said Dad was a changed man and we needed to give him another chance. No surprise that he hadn't changed at all, and in time, she left again. This time it was for good.

I never knew why Dad didn't hit me. I would wonder why he wouldn't just grab me, throw me to the ground and hit me too. I used this invincibility to help my brother.

After my mum and dad had officially separated, my brother and I were staying at Dad's house. Again, Dad randomly flew off the handle at my brother. I ran into the kitchen and stood between my dad and brother, telling my dad to fuck off and that he wasn't going to touch my older brother. I could feel my brother's hands tightly gripping my shoulders as I stood there staring down my dad. No one was going to be getting hurt on my watch.

Situations like this taught me I could be a protector. That I could be the difference in a moment to help another person. This became instinctual, and, in my late teens, I did something similar for a friend when her boyfriend started going off. I ran into the line of fire when everyone else was getting out of the way.

I have always tried to make sense of the world around me. We didn't speak about anything that happened in this secret world that existed behind closed doors. No one listened, anyway. I don't recall ever having a conversation with my mum about what was going on, or if I was okay. It was our normal. We just woke up to a brand-new day and began again like nothing happened. I learnt to accept there was always darkness, even if we didn't understand why. We simply appeared to be at the mercy of life and without the power to change it. I considered what was happening to be neither right nor wrong. All I knew was it felt awful, and I felt helpless.

Our world was shaken when it was discovered my dad had a brain tumour in his frontal lobe, the area of the brain which controls emotions and behaviour. Suddenly, it all made sense. The person we knew wasn't real; he was created from a brain tumour. Confusion and concern filled my brother's and my world as we spent time in the city when Dad was admitted to hospital.

I recall seeing Dad after his operation, with his hair shaved from the hairline to the crown. The dome of his head was stapled back together from where they had cut him open from ear to ear to remove the tumour. He had longer curly hair, so he looked like the creepy clown from Steven King's "IT", except it was my dad. The moment was made lighter by the surgeon's joke that his brain tumour wouldn't even fit into one of our very large vegemite jars; it was the size of a grapefruit! Incredible. How did his brain fit in there, too?

Given this new information, we removed the blame for my dad's behaviour from my dad and placed it on his brain tumour. Mum told my brother and I we needed to forgive him because it wasn't his fault. Easier said than done when you had so many memories and fears that now formed part of your DNA.

Years later, I remember sitting down with Dad as he opened up about how much he regretted that he and Mum had separated, and how he didn't understand why she left. For me, I was wondering why he thought she would stay. I asked him a question, which I spat out more like a statement, "Don't you know what you did!" As it turned out, he had no idea.

All the beatings, all the times he had hurt Mum and my brother both physically and emotionally, he didn't have the slightest idea that anything had happened. It was as if the tumour deleted the memories of every shitty thing he had ever done. It sucked having to be the person to tell Dad why his son despised him and why the love of his life left him, but I guess I was the only one who could.

This showed me I could have hard conversations. A beneficial trait, as a life coach. I have had to learn when and how to use this skill. It has gotten me into trouble at times when people weren't quite ready or wanting to hear my 'wisdom'. So, I learnt when to open my mouth and when to keep it shut.

My life's challenges were not limited to my experiences with Dad…

Growing up, kids don't worry about what is happening behind closed doors. Therefore, the usual bullying and ridicule was still present. I was the fat kid, meaning I was teased a lot, the brunt of bullies' jokes. Often my brother was one of them. Given how my brother was treated at home, it's understandable he tried to obtain a sense of power outside the house. Being the younger sibling, I was the sacrificial lamb receiving the punches. It wasn't until later I acknowledged I was the end of the line. I didn't continue the pattern of being hurt and hurting others. I absorbed it all. Burying the pain deep inside. Failing to believe I was good enough or worthy of being treated better. It was just my turn to receive the beatings and ridicule.

I never discovered a healthy sense of worth growing up. I didn't even know having positive thoughts was a thing. When life was full of lemons, sport was my outlet. Netball, specifically. It provided an escape from 'normal' life. I was a naturally gifted player and umpired as a junior. Later in life, I coached my daughter's teams. Sport gave me a sense of belonging. People wanted me on their team. It was one of the only times I wasn't the last one picked. Unfortunately, this positive outlet ended up with me subconsciously linking my worth to what I could do or be for others. A pattern that continued in all areas of my life for a long time.

When I was a teen, I would clean the house for my Mum on a Saturday morning when she was at work. I just wanted to feel like I had done something right. She was always so grateful. That smile and a hug was worth it every week. Well, until it wasn't.

I don't think you get through life without being hurt by people at one point or another. I remember when I was about twelve waiting for an hour in the rain after netball training for Mum to come and pick me up. By this stage, my younger brother was born. (There's a twelve-year age gap between us.) As I waited, after turning away lifts from others, it became apparent that she had forgotten me. So, I walked home. When I arrived, I noticed one of Mum's friends' cars in the driveway. As I walked in the door, I could hear them laughing and talking. I slammed the door shut and walked into the kitchen where they were sitting. I was met by a look of realisation and apology. Mum tried to explain that my younger brother had fallen asleep, and she didn't want to wake him, then her friend had come around. Being cold, wet and angry, I just turned on my heels and walked away. It was in that moment a seed was sown. I just wasn't important enough or worthy enough to be remembered. I would always be second best. I didn't matter. I confirmed this theory by linking all the moments in time where she had been there for my brothers or for work but not for me. I was always the one that was okay, so never required the additional attention. I just wanted to be seen, and to feel loved and safe. In that moment I decided that was never going to happen.

The moments that involved my Mum hurt so much more because in my eyes, she was the one who was there to protect us. She was the rock when everything else was falling apart. I lost my rock and began to feel like I was on my own.

After I was molested, these beliefs were cemented. It occurred whilst at the beach with a friend. She went down the dunes and I sat on the boardwalk waiting for her. It was a cold, wet day. A man walked up and began talking to me. After a while he said that I looked cold, and he sat behind me with his legs straddling my sides. He then grabbed and played with my breasts. I was 12. Shocked and confused, I eventually told him I had better go and find my friend. As I stood up and began to walk away, he asked, "Am I making you uncomfortable? I thought that's what you wanted." The event made me feel exceptionally vulnerable. What had I done wrong for him to think I wanted that? I was so ashamed of myself. I managed to tell my friend but made her swear not to tell anyone. In my mind, anything that adults did to me was always my fault, and I didn't want to face the embarrassment of what I had done. What would people think and say? Eventually, my friend convinced me to tell her mum. I was unable to recount the event, so she spoke up on my behalf. Before I knew it the police were there, and I was talking to a local police officer. I remember the articles in the local newspaper outlining what had happened to me to warn the public. Advising it wasn't an isolated incident. People on the school bus asked if it was me. Of course, I denied it. I was still so embarrassed and ashamed of my stupidity.

One year later, the police called. They wanted me to look at more images of potential suspects. I was alone as Mum was at work. After I left the police station, I realised I was still struggling with what had happened. When I arrived home, I told Mum I wasn't coping. She turned to me and huffed that I should "just get over it", then walked away. I felt I was alone, and that I didn't matter. She would be there for my brothers, but not for me.

I have discussed this moment with my mum in recent years and explained how much it hurt. Although I have healed beyond the need of an apology, it was nice to receive one, and to hear she was devastated to think she had said that to me. She said she didn't recall the situation, but it was something her own mother would have said to her. A relationship which still burns painfully in her own life. **It never ceases to amaze me how the past becomes the future if you fail to heal and grow beyond life's pain and trauma.** More of which life had in store for me.

Mum would say I woke up on my sixteenth birthday a different person. Gone was the loving, helpful daughter she once had. Instead replaced with the stereotypical "dreaded" teen. I lived a lifetime between sixteen and eighteen. I discovered boys, alcohol, drugs and parties. I rebelled against the world, especially my mum. A switch had been flicked, and I hated her. Instead of seeking comfort from someone safe, I sought out boys to make me feel special. The thing with most teenage boys is they are generally after one thing, and it wasn't to make *me* feel special. I used my body to make me feel loved and wanted. I buried my pain with drugs and alcohol, looking for the immediate high, a way to escape life. Life spiralled out of control. I stopped going to school and eventually signed myself out. I knew I wasn't going to pass my final exams for year eleven, so I couldn't see the point in continuing.

Sixteen was also when I attempted suicide. I didn't want to be here anymore. I hated myself and the world. I grabbed all the painkillers in the house, and I took them, one after the other, until they were gone. I fell asleep that night hoping I would never wake again. The pain which plagued my heart was going to be over.

The relief was short lived.

When I woke up, boy, I felt sick. Only reinforcing that I wished I hadn't woken at all. All the pain killers were gone, and I was still bloody alive. Fuck that! I had experienced enough and wanted out. Yet here I was, taking on another day.

It's strange to be angry about waking up. I later went through a stage of self-harm. Hoping somehow to release the pain inside, as I continued to lose hope in life.

No one knew about this suicide attempt until I was nineteen. I had bought my first house, moved in and I was chatting to Mum, going through some old CDs when I said, "Oh, this is the song I was listening to when I tried to overdose on pain killers." It's strange how easily it came out. I can still hear the words and tune whenever I think about it. Mum grabbed the CD and broke it. I can't even imagine what was going through her mind when she heard those words. It was probably like a dagger straight to the heart. Thanking the grace of God that I was still with her.

All things considered, I probably should be dead. Or maybe it played out exactly how it was supposed to.

After leaving school, there was a stint living in Perth. Mum couldn't handle me anymore, Dad didn't take me in. I made the most of this opportunity to party and mix in all the wrong circles. I ended up kicked out of the house I was renting a room in. I landed back in my hometown. It was at this point Mum made an important choice; to send me to secretarial college, where I was to live with my aunt, uncle and two cousins.

I am so grateful for the opportunity to have lived with my aunty and uncle. It was everything growing up at home wasn't. Stable, loving and encouraging. They weren't living in survival mode. They accepted me.

I don't think I ever allowed myself to feel connected to the family unit which made their home so special. I was still telling myself I was just their niece and cousin. After all, I wasn't lovable or worthy.

Living with my aunt and uncle was a *huge* turning point in my life. There were new possibilities, new people and new things to see and do. I pulled my head in and gave it my all. I felt in control of my life. It's the feeling so many young adults experience when they first move out of home and begin creating their own life. Living outside the confines of their parents' rules. It was my first real sense of freedom with a positive direction. It was exhilarating.

When I first moved in, I changed everything. I was committed to a new me. I was focussed on school, and once I had completed my studies, on work. But this new version of me had a longing for the familiar. I found myself back in the world of drugs, sex and partying, and it drew me in fast. The world I thought I had left behind was again on my doorstep.

It was around this time I met a guy. He wasn't all bad. He was studying at TAFE and had hopes and dreams of his own. A step in the right direction. Well, at least a step up from all the other guys I had previously found myself with.

By this stage I had long moved out of my aunty and uncle's house, and I was renting a room close to the city. I was very much living by my own rules, of which there were apparently very few. Between seventeen and eighteen, life was spiralling out of control again. My eighteenth birthday was ruined by my boyfriend's inability to score drugs. He was unhappy about it and didn't we all know it. Over the year or so I was with him, my Cave continued to form. I still didn't have any self-worth, so I felt as though this guy was the bee's knees. I didn't think I deserved to be treated any better. A special dinner out was him shouting me to a meal combo from Hungry Jacks, and I did feel super lucky to receive that. I ended up moving in with him. As time went on, it became apparent we weren't good for one another. We were smoking way too much pot and there were weeknights when we would use ice, a highly addictive drug, just because we were bored and could.

A few months after my eighteenth birthday, I went to visit Mum in Darwin. It was there I met someone who introduced me to a whole new level of possibility. He opened my eyes, and my heart soon followed.

I was set up on a blind date by Mum. She didn't like my boyfriend—I can now understand why—and was extracting this random new prospect's blood when she told him he should take me out. At this point, I should mention that Mum worked at the Red Cross Blood Service taking blood donations. This poor guy was just doing his act of community service. He wasn't exactly looking for a date. Mum had obviously forgotten all her stranger danger talks and wasn't worried about setting me up with a complete stranger. After all, he ticked all the right boxes during his pre donation interview. If you have ever given blood, you will know just how in-depth this interview is, even down to when was the last time you had a cold or if you have ever slept with prostitutes. Before I knew it, she was calling me, most proud of herself for getting me a date. All I had to do was call him.

I have since learnt the other side of this story, which adds its own element of entertainment. He was thinking I must be a complete nutter, given that my mother was setting me up. He also presumed I was butt ugly, even though my mum had assured him I looked like

Claudia Schiffer. Hmm, not sure about that Mum, but thanks for the compliment. Either way, after some convincing from the guys at work, he decided to do yet another act of public service and take this girl—me—out. Not to blow my own horn, but at the time we met I was a size ten, blonde-haired, blue-eyed, five-foot-eight young lady who, ironically, thought she was the ugliest thing on the planet.

He was the first man to take me out to a proper restaurant for a date. It was on this date that I learnt he really disliked vegetables. I didn't know it then but as it turned out, I would be eating his vegetables for many years to come. This was the night I met my first love, who would become my husband.

This first date led to another three, and with the knowledge that he was moving to Western Australia, which is where I lived, in just a few weeks—it felt like it was meant to be. I was smitten. He took me to explore waterfalls and showed me something I had never experienced before: true connection. By the end of my trip, I didn't want to go home. I cried as I lay on him, telling him as much. If summer love is a thing, then the beginning of our love story was exactly that. The moment I arrived home, I broke up with my boyfriend. Even though it broke his heart, I recognised we weren't good for one another. I had experienced something far greater, and he deserved the opportunity to find that too.

Life between nineteen and twenty-four was great. I bought my first house, was married, fell pregnant with my first child, the second one coming along eighteen months later. Life was great. I ticked lots of major life boxes. Purchasing my first house turned out to be a wonderful investment, increasing to six figures in just over twelve months. This decision alone paid off over and over again and was one of the main reasons I was able to stay home longer with my children. This was all made possible due to the passing of my dad. He died from cancer soon after my nineteenth birthday.

The cancer was everywhere: his liver, brain, lungs, etcetera. It was one month from diagnosis to death, which saw him spend his fiftieth birthday lying in a hospital bed. I completely forgot my own birthday, which is the day after my dad's. I remember sitting with Mum at the train station, waiting for a bus. We randomly ran into my aunt and her twin sister. I turned to Mum and asked what day it was. She looked at me wide-eyed and told me it was my birthday.

Every day I would head to the hospital after work. I would spend time with him, chatting about things, trying not to drown him as I wet his mouth with one of those little sponges on a stick. I could see his body letting him down. He couldn't lift his arms. He became bloated and drawn in the face. These were not things we discussed, unless he was telling me off for a near-drowning experience, that is. We talked about our favourite memories, life, regrets; anything other than death. I was there when the doctors gave him his life expectancy of three months. I wasn't going to waste the little time we had ahead of us. As previously mentioned, three months turned out to be a generous timeframe.

Other than the loss of Dad, the worst thing that happened was my cat dying. His life cut short by his curiosity of a dishwasher. For all of you who are a little intrigued by this: no, he didn't go through a full cycle. It was while I was unstacking the dishwasher, in a rush to meet an appointment on time. I emptied the bottom rack first and didn't see him jump in. Once I had finished unstacking, I shut the door and ran out of the house. That was the end of Ash, and I was heartbroken. The silver lining in this situation is that I ended up with the most beautiful cat, who was with us for sixteen years. He was perfect with the kids, pretty much seeing each of them to sleep at night before joining my husband and me. Upon getting JJ, the new cat, my husband tried to make an ill-timed joke. He said we should call him 'Pyrex'. As in, 'dishwasher safe'. I did not take too kindly to that joke at the time, but now see it was actually pretty clever.

The silver lining does exist when you actively seek it out. Even in our darkest moments, light will always shine, sometimes you just need to keep moving forward to be able to see it. It also never shows up the way you imagine.

The pain and trauma you experience never goes anywhere unless you dig it up, pull it out and have a good look at it, dealing with any of the emotions and beliefs created by them. Like the situation with my mum. It sits there in the depths of our soul, influencing our hearts and minds, often unconsciously.

Although life was going well during my early twenties, all my self-hate and feelings of unworthiness sat simmering under the surface.

Becoming a mother challenged me. It required me to step into learning how to be someone new. No longer were my goals and dreams at the forefront of my focus. Instead, I had this beautiful creation in front of me that grew inside my womb. Again and again, I stepped into what motherhood required of me. I lost myself. I was the perfect mother and wife doing a great job at keeping everything just so. But my spark had gone, and my simmering self-hate began to surface.

It was during the second and third trimester of my second pregnancy that the wheels started falling off and my internal world combusted I would lose myself in my self-hatred. There was one instance where my husband had taken our dogs for a walk with our first child, so I was home alone. I had encouraged them to go, as I was planning on taking a bath. But that wasn't all I had planned. No sooner than I had waved them goodbye, I was into the razors, breaking them open as the bath ran. Here I was with a swollen belly, thinking by the time they arrived home I would be dead, but there would be a chance they would be able to save the baby. I can only assume hormones were the catalyst for this perfect storm, helped along by a lack of sleep and purpose. Luckily, for some reason, my hubby ended up back at home before I had even managed to make the first cut. I still remember the banging on the door as he begged me to let him in.

There are times when I reflect on the lows from which I have risen. I lived deep inside my Cave, and no one knew except for my husband. It seems like a lifetime ago, and so strange that this person was even me. It was in those low points that I was at the very back of my Cave, screaming at anyone who tried to save me. During those dark days, there was only one person who was trying to save me, my husband.

I feel deeply grateful that he stuck by me through those dark times. I owe him my life. I put him through hell. I can only imagine what it would be like to find your very pregnant wife in a bathtub, broken razors all around her, tears streaming down her face, knowing you still have a small child to care for and protect. Over the years we had our challenges, and I am not surprised that there were times he wanted to leave. Ultimately, he did leave. All the drama from my learning and growing took its toll.

For me to grow, I needed to unlearn all the things that I thought I knew about myself. I needed to dig myself out of a momentous pile of shit and rubble that I had piled up on top of me. I needed to forgive horrible people, I needed to reframe things, give new meaning to situations in my life that would allow me to move forward. I needed to seek the silver linings in crappy situations. To start telling myself a new story about myself. But before I could do all that, there were still more challenges to overcome. More circumstances to make me, break me and shape me.

When Dad passed away, I was left with a lot of regret. The night he died I was out letting off steam. I needed a break from hospitals, and I figured that one night out would be okay. I was wrong. Dad was in the hospital in our hometown, so I ran into old school friends when I was out drinking. Late in the night, Mum began trying to call me. I was somewhat drunk and had been smoking pot and I didn't want her to know, so I didn't answer. After about the tenth call, I finally picked up. That was when I learnt Dad wasn't going to make it through the night. Mum instructed me to grab my older brother from the house and get to the hospital. Luckily, a friend was able to drive. We went to get my brother. He didn't want to come, so we left him. After a quick pit stop for the driver to buy some cigarettes, we found ourselves at the hospital. A nurse was waiting for me at the door to let me in. The first thing she said was, "I'm so sorry, he's gone." I fell to my knees right there in the doorway and cried. I was too late. I had put myself and my needs first, and I wasn't there at the last moment.

The following days were a blur. Mum arrived from interstate and the funeral was planned. At that stage there was a lady friend in Dad's life. Not a girlfriend, but someone I guess he wanted to ensure was cared for. So, he made allowances in his will for her to stay in his house for twelve months after his passing. As it turns out, she was a horrible person. She turned Dad's passing into a rather shitty situation. You see, with this lady and her father, Dad had made a will that left her with more time in the house and more allowances. Dad felt he had made a mistake, so arranged for another will to be made with his true final wishes.

To cut through much of the story: money went missing, she didn't look after the house, she sold many of Dad's belongings in a garage sale and took anything else she wanted. Even with all this, I still feel the worst thing she did was when it came to spreading Dad's ashes. After all, the other things were just that—things. My older brother and I had organised to stay at the house with her, and she had agreed to it. We were unaware of what she was up to at that point. The day before the spreading of the ashes, I called to confirm our arrival time. My brother and I were already on route when she turned around and said no, we couldn't stay. We were shocked and had to come up with a Plan B, which was to stay with one of the executors of Dad's will, who was one of his best friends. He said it was okay, but he mentioned that he spoke to the lady in Dad's house, and that she said we never organised to stay at the house. She had made us out to be lying and just wanting to be difficult. We told our side of the story, but it was always going to be her word against ours.

The best part about spreading the ashes is that Dad must have been there in spirit with a cheeky sense of vengeance. He wanted his remains cast out at his favourite fishing spot. Boats had been arranged and we did just that. All went well, and no random wind blew his remains into our faces. The giggles came when it was time to get out of the boats and back onto dry land. Now, this lady was a much bigger lady and was in a different boat to my brother and me. As she got out of the boat, her short legs didn't make it overly well and she fell face-first into the water. I stifled my laugh, but I tell you what—it serves her right. You would be correct in thinking that I'm not a fan of this person. I won't be inviting her over for a cup of tea any time soon, that's for sure. She left empty shoe boxes and all her new purchase wrappings for us to find, along with dead mice in cupboards. Mum and I cleaned the house once she had left. There was no consideration for us as she took off in her new car and camper, presumably bought with the money Dad had told Mum was hidden in cash for my brother and me.

At the time Dad passed, all that remained of his side of the family was my grandfather. Given our Dutch heritage we called Dad's dad "Opah". My brother and I were his only surviving family here in

Australia. My Uncle had committed suicide when I was about ten. My grandmother, or "Omah", died a few years later after a battle with cancer. Then my dad. Opah was miserable, as was to be expected. My older brother would go see him regularly and I would send him letters every month, visiting whenever I returned to Perth. I had moved to Darwin after Dad passed to live closer to Mum.

Not too long after the birth of my second daughter, I began noticing that Opah kept saying he wished he could help but he didn't have any money. I wasn't looking to get handouts, so it seemed strange for him to mention it. Opah had some mental health problems, so after Omah passed, a friend from the church was arranged to become his power of attorney. This individual turned out to be a right piece of work. He took and hid my opah's car when we were trying to transport my dying father home. He kicked my brother out of my opah's house because he had bought it, which was news to us, and never offered us the contents of the property. He was cunning. So, given what my opah was saying, warning bells began to sound.

Before Opah passed, I went through the State Administration Tribunal—a formal mediation process—to have his power of attorney revoked and arranged to have Opah's finances put into the hands of the Public Trustee. During the hearings which proceeded, an audit confirmed that this church-going fella had not been squandering Opah's funds. This was great news, but my gut kept telling me that wasn't the end of the story. The truth of his long-term plan came out once Opah died.

Call me what you like, the day Opah passed, I was ready for action. I cleared out his room at the nursing home and began organising his possessions. I delayed my grieving for what ended up being years. I could smell the fish, and I wanted to be ready. So, I contacted a lawyer. The man wouldn't show us Opah's will, so my lawyer arranged to get hold of it by court order. The news shouldn't have cut me off at the knees, but it did. Upon hearing what was in the will, I broke a little more. Again, we would have to fight for what was rightfully ours. The will had smaller sums going to close friends, which I had no problem with. My brother and I were left ten thousand dollars each and the ex-power of attorney was to inherit the rest, which was in the ballpark of hundreds of thousands of dollars. As much as I died a little more inside, I put on the boxing gloves and prepared to fight. I am not an unfair person. I understood and acknowledged that this person was there for my opah and had done much for him. He deserved something for the years of friendship, but to take the major portion? This was taking advantage of my opah's situation, neurological condition and emotional stress. After all, this guy already had his house, car and possessions.

Beginning the process of contesting Opah's will, Mum, my

brother and I agreed no matter what the outcome, my brother and I would evenly split the outcome.

Growing up, my older brother had turned more and more towards living inside of his own Cave. He was getting into so much strife with drugs, to the point where he spent time in jail. He was diagnosed with drug induced schizophrenia. My brother had spent his entire life running from what had happened to him as a kid. He never had the opportunity to yell at Dad for what had happened.

My brother never had to show up to meetings with lawyers, or the days in negotiation. He never even had to look at the legal paperwork or pay the legal bills. Yet when all was said and done, and he learnt that he could be given a greater share, he took the opportunity. Again, I was shafted. This time by my own family. To make matters worse, Mum never stood up for what was agreed. At that time, Mum was my brother's power of attorney and was required to report my brother's finances to the Public Trustee, as he was deemed unfit to manage his own finances. As there was a significant difference between the two payouts, she didn't want to get in trouble if they didn't see a private agreement as fit reason for the withdrawal. I get it, but man did this dagger hurt like hell. After breaking the news to me, my lawyer asked me if I wanted to fight it. Through my dismay, I responded no. I wasn't prepared to waste any more money on a lost cause. Fighting had already cost me so much.

Now, that included a piece of my heart.

This case really sucked the wind from my sails. At the time, I had a full-time job, and my husband had just landed one as well since our move to Western Australia. I ended up quitting my job because I couldn't cope with the requests and requirements of home, the case, myself, the job, and everything else that life was throwing at me. All the stress finally led me to seeking professional help for the first time. I was incredibly broken walking into that psychiatrist's office and to tell you the truth, they didn't help very much. The anti-depressants just made me feel like crap. I was still dealing with self-hate and feeling disconnected from life. But I forced myself to keep getting out of bed. Some days were a real struggle.

I remember one day my husband called Mum to come talk to me, because he was worried about me. I was again refusing to get out of bed. Mum came over. She walked into the room. We had a brief conversation, in which I told her I was just tired. She walked out, told my husband that I was just tired, and left. I was surprised it was that easy to pull the wool over her eyes. Knowing what I do now, I realise she probably couldn't even see past everything that was going on with her, let alone be there for me in the way that I required her to be.

I have had more than enough reasons not to have my family in my life. I could have found enough weight from heartache alone to walk away. Ultimately, this is not what I wanted. Having already lost Dad assisted the decision to reconcile. Inner strength, combined with a willingness to forgive, transformed the situation. Life has taught me that holding onto pain and suffering is easier in the short term but will affect your life negatively in the long term. It's the exact opposite of the way I want to live my life. I would also like to note here that forgiveness needs to come with a warning label. **Some people are not deserving of complete forgiveness. Without a change in behaviour, they continue to hurt you in the same way.** I have experienced and seen this so many times. I hoped someone would change and they didn't. They chose who they wanted to be. Sometimes I wonder if I'm too hard on people. Too cutthroat. Then I remember I am truly deserving. I don't settle. Not for family and not to keep someone else happy.

I am pleased to say, that this is pretty much the end of the major drama. From this point on it was the usual stuff, me kicking my brother out of my house, other general family drama, and arguing with my stepdad over various matters.

My brother continued his downward spiral, and there were times I was left to clean up the mess he left behind. When my brother first went to jail, my stepdad refused to clean up his own house. The gardens had been left untouched for months. Mum worked away and asked if I would clean everything up for her. Emotionally, this felt like the last straw. Boy was I angry, weeds as tall as a four-wheel drive. I pulled them out and cried. I yelled at the leftovers of my brothers 'friends'—who popped over to score—to piss off. I was always the one who cleaned up the mess and I was sick of it. Mum may have paid me to do this for her, but it took a big emotional toll.

By the time the legal battle with Opah's estate was done and dusted, I was about thirty. I felt as if I had lived and experienced all that life had to throw at a person. Internally, I was shattered, and I didn't think that I mattered. I believed all I was good for was getting stuff done and solving problems. I could be a good Mum, if providing basic needs counted. I look at the love I offered my children back then and I now see it was conditional. When I first recognised this, I would get wrapped up in wanting to go back and change things. Now I know I'm not perfect. I'm learning and growing. I simply live for today and plan for tomorrow. It doesn't matter what happened yesterday. It's how I show up today that counts.

It has taken time for me to learn how to give myself unconditional love. To believe I am deserving of having it all, and not expect anything less. To love me exactly as I am, even on the days I feel low and uninspired. The way I treat myself, my finances, my body and my mind are all important. The way I *allow* people to treat me teaches them how to *treat* me. It is through learning how to give myself unconditional love that I learnt how to give it to others. This journey has not only made me a better person; it made me a better mother.

For so long, I was addicted to my story. Sharing was a way of getting significance. "Look at what I have been through, it was so much worse than you. You're so lucky and I am strong, just let me prove it by telling you even more." Spew face 🤮 emoji. It is also why I needed to really check in as to what benefit sharing my story in this book would provide.

For a long time, I felt I had no control over what showed up in my life. I was simply a victim to whatever life wanted to throw at me. My point of view was that life happened to you. Swim like hell or you will drown. Protect yourself in every way possible. Build walls for others to climb over. Add extra walls to ensure your safety. Be cautious of everyone. Don't trust anyone, not even yourself.

When my marriage ended, it shook my world to the core. It made me question everything. Who I was, my goals and dreams, the people around me? I forgot the life I had been working towards. I had to start again from the ground up. I think the hardest part about a separation is learning how to start again.

You argue about the old things. You argue about the things that keep you connected, such as kids. Amongst all of that is discovering who you are in your new circumstances.

I had to let go of the old habits of a married woman. Including how I gave love. The love I use to give to a partner, I had to figure out what to do with it. I eventually learnt that I could give it to myself or whoever else I chose. I redefined the direction of my life. Well, once I worked out what that was. I began to build a life for myself and my girls. I learnt a hell of a lot about myself and what I could achieve. I discovered beliefs I held about myself that kept me small and insignificant. I challenged those beliefs. I redesigned myself in every way when my marriage ended.

I look back on his decision to leave with awe. It was a brave decision to end it. I wouldn't be the person I am today without him making that call. I learnt so much about myself and what I wanted. I was also free to chase and do whatever I wanted. I became more self-assured, confident, resilient and independent. I know what I want, and I have achieved goals which I wasn't sure I was able to pull off, especially on my own. I dared to be brave. **My world expanded because he made the decision to leave.** How can I *not* be grateful for the opportunity to have more of myself? I learnt unconditional love by giving myself what I needed. I didn't wait to receive it from someone else. I became complete on my own.

Strength was born out of the darkness. Resilience out of the times that almost broke me. Love was discovered through finding me.

The Cave was once a sanctuary, a place to hide from and store the barrage of shit from the outside world. Then the darkness found its way into the Cave. It tried to swallow me whole. Finding myself was the key to discovering the light. It didn't always come easy. There were times I needed to dig deep into the depths of my soul to find the courage to pick myself up and dust off. Each of these falls left scars. I became the courageous character who fights between good and evil, who continues to stand up even when bruised, bloodied and beaten. This character possesses everything we desire for ourselves. Faith, hope and trust.

It's beautiful that we can all find ourselves in this character. When you cannot see beyond where you are, you generally find yourself filled with uncertainty and, at times, fear. What you must realise is this is completely normal, and, in many respects, it makes life so much more interesting. Imagine if you chose to see the uncertainty as an adventure that you were excited to explore, rather than fearing the unlimited possibility. Your mind can be your greatest asset or your greatest liability. Fighting yourself is often harder than fighting the devil itself.

The saying that life happens *for* you, not *to* you, rings very true these days. Challenges are here to teach. I have learnt to look for the silver lining. To find a way back to forgiveness and love so my soul can be content.

What are the things I learnt which made all the difference?

Read on, my fellow life adventurer. The keys to unlocking the magic are ahead of you.

2 – It All Starts With a Wake-up Call

In one way or another, we are all seeking greater meaning in life. Most of us just don't know where to start looking. This is where the wake-up call comes into play. It is that thing which inspires us. Ignites the fire within us to be and experience life in a greater way. Often, we don't recognise what it is until we have stepped onto the path. It is the process of awakening the soul and freeing the mind.

When I look back at my wake-up call, I can't say that it was anything earth-shattering. It really was quite ordinary. For me, it was the realisation that I didn't have to be at the mercy of people and situations in my life. It was the awareness that I had more of a say in how life panned out.

There are a lot of haters when it comes to network marketing. Yet from a personal development standpoint, it was the best bloody thing I ever did. I didn't make a cracker, but it introduced me to the world of personal development. At the time, I believed personal development was for those who were really screwed up. What I didn't know was that *I* was completely screwed up. That's what we call dramatic irony.

On a trip to a conference, my friend who introduced me to network marketing spoke about creating your own life. She told me about this book called *The Secret* and this magical thing called the Law of Attraction. You can only imagine what my face looked like when she said this. Everything I understood about the world at this point was that I was not in control. Now here was this person telling me the complete opposite.

I read the book, and my mind was blown. If I simply thought about something enough, the universe would conspire, and it would show up. This information inspired me. It led me into a whole lot of thinking about stuff, and to some small degree, it worked. For the big things like business success, however, that didn't seem to work quite so well. I read all the books in the series, making notes and doing all the activities, looking for that missing piece. Why, with all this thinking, was it not just showing up?

It was around this time I met another person who was in the network marketing game, who introduced me to more books on the law of attraction. This was when I became aware of the internal journey that was also required, and I was all in. I embraced it all because I wanted to be a success and take control of my life. I didn't want to be at the mercy of life anymore. I knew I could create the outcomes in my life. That knowledge thrilled me.

The funny side of all of this is that I spent much time thinking about everything that I desired, imagining I already had all the success, money, freedom, etcetera. I thought so hard, I am sure I ended up with more furrows on my forehead. Then I discovered the next piece of the puzzle. This was a ground-breaking moment for me, almost like a second wake-up call. I needed to take action. To actually do something to make it happen. To show the universe I wanted it.

From this point forward, I had the aim of mastering the law of attraction. To have the life I wanted. What I didn't realise was that I would end up living a life full of love, laughs, and all-consuming happiness. For so many of you reading this, it may seem like a tall tale. But if you have happiness, love and joy in your life—well, you already have it all. Everything else will always fall into place perfectly, at the perfect time.

For me, learning I was in control was empowering. No longer was my power being taken away from me. For the first time in my life, it felt like life was truly in my hands.

It was scary because I knew things had to change. At the same time, it was exciting. My heart called out to me with a strength I never knew it had, and my eyes shone a little brighter from the embers that began to burn in my soul.

There are periods in your life when things are going great. Then something happens to crush you like a tonne of bricks. You end up bruised and battered, and that's okay. Each beating is an opportunity to grow, and that is the true intention behind the challenge. There are also moments where life is going wonderfully, and then it becomes even better. Expect this also. It is not always a case of being too good to be true. Maybe life can be that grand and easy. It will twist and turn for both the better and worse, that is what life is about. Each gift and challenge, a marvellous opportunity to grow and connect to even more of ourselves and the world.

Each of us is here for a reason. From where you are right now, you may not know what the end game is. I can't help but believe there is one. **You are a rare and intricate gift. It is miraculous that you're here.**

If there were no such thing as a coincidence, if everything and everyone happened for a reason, what would that change for you?

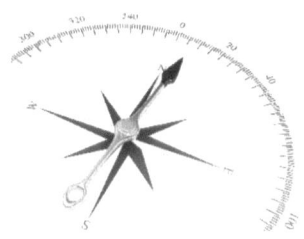

3 - Gratitude

Gratitude is no longer a new concept. Most of us have heard of it in one way, shape or form. It can be easy to find in some situations, and hard to connect with in others. **The process of introducing and applying gratitude has the capacity to dramatically transform your life.**

Change your mindset to an attitude of gratitude. Be thankful for what you have in your life. You might focus on the things you like, but you can delve deeper into gratitude. This involves taking something you're less than happy with and finding a way to be thankful for it. The most important thing is not to focus on the negative. Focus on the positive instead.

For some people, developing and expressing gratitude can feel like a bit of a minefield, especially if it's towards a person who has hurt you. So, why would I want to be grateful towards someone like this, I hear you ask. This is the healing journey. To express gratitude in these instances, you need to first forgive. To offer a broader perspective: forgiveness is selfish. Hear me out. To forgive someone means you are no longer allowing what that person did to you to affect you. As a result, you take back your personal power. If you're reacting to situations in a particular way due to past experiences, you are giving people power over how you show up today.

Without awareness in your actions, the way you react may not be in alignment with who you want to be. If you have children, it's like the times you've gone nuts at them and it wasn't necessary. I have done this more times than I care to admit. One such time, I was driving in the car and the kids were arguing about pointless things. The day had been quite stressful for me, so my emotions popped. I yelled at them to stop annoying one another and I mean, really yelled. I blamed them for all of the little things they had done over the past few months which hadn't taken my needs into consideration. I tried to make them feel awful because, in that moment, I was feeling awful about myself and the stresses I was experiencing.

Ultimately, this is not the type of parent I want to be. When I do go nuts, I apologise and explain why I reacted that way. I also make a point of telling them that I am going to learn from the situation. Then I change my behaviour. The whole point of this is to show them how to learn and grow emotionally from a relatively normal situation. I am not perfect. The beautiful thing I have learnt from doing this is that kids are pure unconditional love. The smaller, the purer. I usually get a big cuddle. Sometimes, I will then talk about their behaviour. I ask them how they could have reacted better. They're not perfect, either. This provides the opportunity for everyone to learn and grow.

By challenging perfectionism and embracing the world of growth, your words and actions become your child's foundation. They're learning how to behave by watching you. You're showing them that it's okay to screw up. To get grumpy. The world is full of attempts at perfectionism. Let kids see that even adults screw up, and that nothing will implode if they do. Also let them to see you succeed. Share your wins. Be the tall poppy. Children pay attention more than we ever give them credit for, even when they don't show it. They're creating their own meanings and learning how to react to situations from watching and listening to you. Teach them humility and how not to be perfect. Just to be their best self, even when they get it wrong. It's called being human. Let's allow them to be human also.

I am open about my life's journey to my kids. I want them to see that there are good times and bad times, and that's normal. The biggest thing I want to teach my kids is for them to know that they can handle anything. Isn't this what the role of a parent is? To empower kids so they're prepared for the real world. We forget that it's *their* life journey, and apart from giving them the necessities of life, we need to provide a space for them to explore and get shit wrong. They need the opportunity to screw up, so they too learn resilience and challenge perfectionism. To know that when things do go wrong—and they will—they can back themselves and deal with it and not make the problem bigger. Ironically, you must first empower yourself by giving yourself permission to do the same. In doing so, you will lay the path for them to follow. Alas! I have digressed. So, let's return to the topic of this chapter.

Gratitude assists in putting things into perspective. It can make big problems feel small. Or give hope that things will get better. Or that life isn't as bad as we like to think sometimes. Gratitude isn't something you just say or do, it is meant to be *felt*. It's a feeling, or energetic flow, which goes out into the world and brings back more of what you are grateful for. If you are unsure how to feel gratitude, take the time to consider what would happen if you were to lose your job. What would be the financial impact? How would this affect you and your family? Consider when you have been terribly ill or injured at some point. Did you take a moment to think, 'I will never take my health for granted again'? Then, as with most good things, over time you forget this promise to yourself. You forget to appreciate your health. I don't often recommend negative thinking. But this type of thinking opens the mind to reasons you could be truly grateful for things, such as your job, people, your health, and so on.

Gratitude is not limited. It can be spread everywhere, in every way imaginable. Clean running water and education are not easily accessible to everyone, and this is something us privileged folk often take for granted. Gratitude may not be able to solve world hunger, but it could inspire you to volunteer or to assist humanity in a smaller, though still impactful, way.

I started a gratitude journal when I first began implementing gratitude in my day-to-day life. It was a structured way to get into the habit of it. I would write ten different things every day that I could be grateful for, aiming never to repeat something I had previously written. Sounds easy enough, but after about two weeks, I started to run out of ideas. I was even grateful for my big toe at one point, due to its ability to keep me standing upright. Other days, I chose to be grateful for the crappy things that occurred the previous day, and the opportunities they created for me to learn and grow.

Never underestimate the power of this simple tool. It is often the simplest of things which can have the greatest impact on our lives. Connecting with gratitude takes you away from being a victim in life and into the space of greater possibility. I cannot recommend it enough, keeping a gratitude journal. Even for just thirty days. Write ten things every day you are grateful for. At the end of the thirty days, you will have 300 things written.

After writing each day, ruminate on every item and cultivate the feeling of gratitude. Feel your heart open and expand for each thing. Allow that feeling to grow exponentially all around you and out into the world.

When you are short for ideas, consider this game: If you could only take with you the things you expressed gratitude for into the following day, what would you be grateful for? What people, events and things could you be grateful for today that would make your tomorrow even more amazing?

Integrating gratitude has taken more than thirty days, it has been years of reminding myself of the person I want to be. And on the days I find my mind in a loop of complaining, reminding myself to refocus on the positive things in my life. Replacing anger—towards others and myself—with forgiveness and love. Gratitude has meant I don't have to judge everything anymore, including myself. I choose to see the world from a broader perspective. Gratitude has allowed me to see greater possibilities for myself and others.

When you're experiencing joy and happiness, this state puts you in alignment with your higher self. You're not supposed to be stressed out, angry, and depressed all the time. Life is supposed to be fun. Yes, there are times it kicks your ass, and you will need to work hard. Other times you will be able to take a more balanced approached. My angels are always with me, reminding me I can achieve anything. Yet another blessing to be grateful for.

Gratitude encourages you to be present. Life can be busy, unpredictable, stressful and full of challenges. When you're grateful for the simple things—a beautiful flower, the sun on your face, a glass of cool water—your focus shifts from being in constant search of things outside of you to seeking contentment and connection from within. This allows you to slow down and quiet the mind. To breathe deeply and fall into flow with life again.

Over the years, I have become more grateful for myself, my life, and the people in it. Life has improved as a result. I wholeheartedly believe the universe loves a grateful heart. Incredible people have shown up in places I never expected. Opportunities have appeared with perfect timing. I am constantly amazed by how abundantly the world shows up for us when we allow it to. For it to do so, we must be focused on the positive, be present, and be grateful, even in the challenging times.

When my husband left me and started dating a friend, people were amazed that I didn't hate this person. I didn't want hatred to guide my behaviour. It wasn't going to create situations and moments that in a year's time, I wouldn't be proud of myself for. Some days were hard. One day, I was in the school sick bay crying my eyes out during a school sports carnival. It was the first public event I had seen them at together. I allowed my emotions to flow, being present with myself. I needed to let go and forgive for me. This meant feeling the emotion. Then letting it all go. Kind of like the ritual of floating a deceased loved one down a river. You cry as the body floats away, taken by the river. It's a symbolic gesture of letting go. This was all about stepping into and being the person I wanted to be. Continuing to love and be forgiving. Opting to seek a greater perspective that provided my heart with comfort during those hard times. This did mean I hid away for many years, protecting my heart and mind. But I grew strong and reappeared a completely new person. I believe, a better person.

When you operate your life without judgment, anger or sadness, you can truly open your heart and mind. No longer do you have enemies. Just people you may not choose to spend time with. Gratitude expands your heart and fills you with the most delicious energy. It's almost like a sweet orgasm that ripples through every cell in your body and makes you warm from the inside out. Or like hot chocolate on a cold, star-filled night. It is delectable and incredibly rewarding.

Gratitude enriches your life. It improves relationships. Encourages you to be present and flow with life. It turns you into a kinder, more connected person. It asks for nothing in return, just acknowledgement. It improves your life in every way. It is the softness and authenticity of your soul.

So why wouldn't you want to feel great with gratitude? Take the thirty-day challenge and discover all the wonderful things in your life that you can be grateful for.

4 - The Ego

Your ego comprises two sides: a negative side and a beneficial side. The ego gets a bad rap. But there are benefits to it. When you're growing, the ego can assist you to step into the new version of yourself as you unbecome everything you were told you were supposed to be. I used mine a lot in my early days of growing.

When you first step out of your Cave, you're seeking certainty and safety. There can be a lot of fear. One way to combat this fear is to step into and utilise your ego. Operating from the ego is generally abrupt. It can be described as having a false sense of confidence. It's like going into the ring swinging before you even see your opponent. **The ego provides a buffer between who you want to be and the world around you. You use the ego to protect yourself from any negative flack the world may want to throw.** You are yet to feel safe and secure in this new version of yourself. Therefore, you become a very forceful version. Your *actions* are trying to prove that *you* have nothing to prove.

For me, when I began telling myself a new story about being worthy and deserving, it was a natural transition to step into the ego. As much as it may not have been the most resourceful first step, it provided me with the knowledge that it's okay to believe in myself. Providing opportunities to learn from getting it wrong. It doesn't matter whether it's business or personal. Stop judging yourself and begin to look at life more objectively. You can use the good and bad results of decisions as a way of testing and measuring if what you're doing is working to achieve a desired outcome.

Believing in yourself can be scary, but it's also a necessary step. I promise that the more you do it, the more comfortable you will become with it. Believing in yourself with ferocity, despite the thoughts and opinions of others, is necessary to achieving anything. Not everyone will agree with your choices. You need to be prepared for the pushback. This is where the negative aspect of the ego is highly beneficial. It encourages you to throw caution to the wind and stand behind what you truly desire. When you feel you need to stand up for doing what you want, your ego will say things like, 'I don't care, I'm going to do it anyway.' Or in relation to success, 'You don't like me doing this because you don't want me to be successful, Well, screw you! I'm going to do it anyway!' It's about saying, 'No matter what they think, this is important, and I need to do this for me.' Another great example is if someone says you can't do something and you think to yourself, 'You just watch me.'

Playing with the ego can be fun. Many people have an alter ego or state of being they step into when they are required to do something they find uncomfortable or fear. The alter ego assists them with doing what is required despite the fear. Beyonce had Sasha Fierce as an alter ego for performances, and I am certain many other famous faces would have an unstoppable version of themselves.

Fear is closely linked with the ego. They tend to show up together. Fear triggers the ego into action because its role is to keep you safe. Two peas in a pod, so to speak. What you have done one hundred times before is familiar and safe. But doing anything new or approaching it in a different way causes fear. The ego wants to keep you doing what you have always done. Challenging the fear and therefore the ego may require you to give yourself a pep talk. To tell yourself that it's ok to try new things when you want a different outcome. Albert Einstein is quoted as saying, "Insanity is doing the same thing over and over again and expecting a different result." Part of taking control of my life, and therefore my behaviour, was becoming aware of my greatest fears and their associated stories. I needed to become clear on why I wanted certain outcomes and why I didn't think I would achieve them. I listed all the excuses why I didn't believe I would be successful. Ultimately, I had a huge fear of success. It is strange that at times, the things we desire most are the things we fear most.

We tend to have a deep knowing or awareness that facing our fears is going to change everything: our financial situation, the dynamic of our relationships, how people interact with us. There will usually be a higher demand put on our time, energy, and efforts. This creates uncertainty. If fear were a cake, these demands would be the key ingredients. **It's the desire for certainty and control over your life that causes the unsettled feeling in your stomach when you begin to change.**

I have a lot of respect for those who continue to strive for success. They have faced judgement, failure, uncertainty. Often for several years preceding what we see as their breakthrough to success. I spent years never giving up on my dream—to create a life of helping others and getting paid for it—whilst staying authentic to me and my heart.

The times I tried network marketing on for size, I learnt a lot. One of the things that got my attention was that as great as the products were, they did not sit well with my soul. My dreams were about my own creations, not someone else's. Making the decision to quit was hard. What if the success I was hoping for was just around the corner and I was walking away just before the finish line? Ironically, it's this same thought process that pushed me through the years of sticking with my business. It made me look at parts of myself I may not have delved into. An example of this was noticing that I was determining my self-worth by how many likes I would get on a post. **Your worth should never be determined by something outside of you.** I was looking at the likes as an indication of who was getting my message, who truly understood and was hearing what I had to say.

What's different now, even though it is still about numbers and people, is that I have the firm belief that those who require my assistance will find me. I have unique gifts that other coaches or energetic healers don't have. I have my knowledge and experience. As I grow, this will change and evolve. Do I still fear success? Not as much as I used to. The uncertainty has its moments ,especially when there's higher levels of uncertainty in other areas of my life. I remind myself to swap those feelings for excitement. I accept whatever shows up, whether I like it or not, which isn't always easy.

Swapping fear for excitement is a conscious choice. Physiologically, you experience these two feelings in the same way. The quickened heart rate, sweaty palms, adrenaline pumping. So, are you experiencing fear or are you just excited? It all comes down to the story you're telling yourself. It's a cognitive shift, of which you become very aware. I will notice the feelings within my body. Then I observe my thoughts. Is it a fear-based story, or empowering?

A fear-based story will be something along the lines of "I can't do that because of this" or "people will reject me if I do this". These stories will always be linked to a false belief, an example of the ego playing games to keep you "safe".

Beyond belief is uncertainty. And remember, the ego does not like uncertainty. It would rather you continue to do what is tried and tested. This steers you away from the unknown to where all the magic and growth occurs.

To make the shift between fear and excitement, you must tell yourself the exact opposite of the fear-based belief or story. If you're worried about people rejecting you, you can use the harsher aspects of ego to your advantage. Instead, say to yourself, 'People will always make choices based on their own perspective. This has nothing to do with me. To live my best life, this is what I am choosing for me.' This is a powerful shift because it screams of self-confidence and certainty. Even if you don't believe it initially, you can grow into the statement. The universe loves this type of definitive choice. Through these clear decisions, the universe will start pulling in the people and situations required to make this choice a reality for you. It's up to you to notice these opportunities and grab them. Just keep stepping into the new belief, challenging the old fear-based one until it is no longer part of who you are.

When it comes to personal development, you need to give yourself permission to screw up. You tend to do it wrong before you learn a better way. It is through screwing it up and losing your shit that you can step into a more resourceful version of yourself. Every time you do this, you will challenge your ego and provoke fear.

Once you begin to see the possibility in the world, you feel a little braver and more confident about stepping out into the sunlight, even if you still have to shield your eyes from the sun's rays at first. This is why the fact that I was in control of what showed up in my life was so ground-breaking for me to discover. In a world where choice didn't seem to exist, other than what I was going to cook for dinner that night, I suddenly had a world of possibilities available to me, where even my wildest dreams could be actualised. On the other side of the coin, it also required me to take responsibility for my life and behaviours.

As a people pleaser, I can't say going against my ego was an easy process. My normal go-to was to make everyone else happy first. My growth point was to put myself first. I didn't want to hurt anyone or have others dislike me. I was still a timid little kitten when I exited my Cave, eyes darting left and right, senses heightened, looking for danger. Going against the side of my ego which wanted to keep me safe. Utilising the false self-belief part of my ego played an important role in my growth. It helped me to create the evidence that I was worthy of whatever I wanted to pursue. Not everyone would agree, and that was okay. Those who were meant to be in my life would stand by my side. Others wouldn't stay the path. People come and go. The purpose is not for everyone to stay for the duration.

There will come a time in your journey when you recognise it's time to give up the ego. The ego shouldn't be held onto in the long term. Its harsh nature can get you into trouble while it tries to keep you safe from uncertainty and fear. Ultimately, its continued presence will keep you closed to new possibilities and holding onto those same fears and uncertainty. As a result, you will not be growing. Eventually, you must seek the softness that love and kindness provide. The ego can cause you to lose friendships due to the "my way or the highway" approach it encourages. Build true self-worth, and you won't require the ego anymore. Imagine a world where love, gratitude and kindness are not the exception. Where everyone has an innate knowledge of their own worth without needing to prove themselves. I believe much of the world would look different. Peace could be achieved on a much larger scale. Even the environment would benefit because people would show gratitude for the resources of the land by caring for and appreciating it.

5 - Listen to Understand

Have you ever found yourself in this situation: You're having a deep and meaningful with a friend, but before you can finish, they interrupt you to give all their well-intended advice? Or maybe you're the guilty party? I know I have been a few times in the past.

When the overwhelming urge to interrupt occurs, it's the mind and ego screaming, 'I have something of value to add!' If it's not shared in that exact moment, it seems the information will be lost forever. At times, you're bouncing up and down on the spot with excitement to share. When you're in this state, you forget to listen. You're so wrapped up in sharing your piece of gold and not forgetting what it is, you forget why you are having the conversation in the first place. It wasn't to share your wisdom. The purpose of the conversation was for your friend to be heard.

The funny thing is that the advice you're planning on sharing is only relevant to you. It's based on your own personal journey and what *you* have learnt and experienced. Your advice may be completely irrelevant to your friend in their life. This can be hard to wrap your head around. What has assisted you in the past may or may not be relevant to your friend's circumstance.

To provide some context, have you ever been given advice that felt disjointed? In other words, it wasn't relevant for one reason or another, even though it seemed on topic. Often, the advice provided doesn't take into consideration all the pieces of the puzzle—the minor complexities which make the issue specific to you. It kind of puts you off sharing the rest of the problem, especially when they are passionate about their advice.

Your advice could be received in the same way. Getting so wrapped up in the delivery, therefore failing to notice how what you're sharing is being received by the other party. Have their eyes glazed over, or do you still have their attention?

This is a trait of the person who tries to "fix" everything. Someone has a problem and just wants to vent, but before they can even finish, the fixer—with the best of intentions—arrives on their fine steed to save the day with all the problem-solving ideas. The person with the problem may be thinking, 'Shut up and just listen.' Oh, and how often does this then become the beginning of an argument? The "fixer" is frustrated, the horse limp, and the person with the problem now has even more ammunition for feeling angry, this time with a new target. The irony in this situation is that the argument occurs due to neither party feeling as if they have been heard.

It all comes down to the importance of listening. To understand what is going on for the person, rather than trying to be the white knight on a limp horse.

Understanding your role within a conversation is essential to having meaningful relationships and connections. Keep in mind that sometimes your role within life does not dictate your position within a conversation. This is a situation I often face with my mum. I begin to share a problem I am experiencing, and she is very quick to offer solutions. She feels as though, as a mum, her life experience has provided her with sufficient knowledge to fix problems. But we look at the world in different ways and have healed to different levels of understanding. I often find her advice lacking in particular areas. This is not a criticism of her and where she is on her journey. Rather, it reminds me that not everyone is best placed to assist us with our life hiccups. Ultimately, it all comes back to listening, rather than rushing to share advice.

When you listen and then ask relevant questions at the appropriate time, you allow the individual to explore relevant solutions from their own life. Asking questions such as, 'What could you do to overcome this?' gets the individual thinking about solutions rather than focusing on the problem. It provides them with an opportunity to explore the experiences from their life and find solutions that would work for them specifically.

Use words meaningfully. You may find, as you become the active listener in a conversation, that you don't speak half as much and may gain more from the conversation. You notice a lot of things when you listen and ask relevant questions. To be honest, this is what life coaches do: allow the individual to connect with their inner wisdom. When you step into being an active listener, you generally become labelled as a good listener. The individual is usually grateful for the conversation, too. Now with strategies they came up with that they can implement. In the end, you really don't have to do anything, just be present and curious.

With all this said, one question has still not been answered: When is it okay to share advice? The answer is simple: When the person asks for it.

Sometimes, despite best efforts, the person has no idea which way to turn to overcome their problem. Questions such as 'What would you do?' or 'Can you give me advice?' are clear indications that your advice is being sought. It really is that simple. Unless you are asked, actively listen and be the best listener you can be in the moment. Be present for the individual in front of you.

6 - Friends, Family, and the Lessons We Learn

"Some people are in our lives for a long time, some people are in our lives for a short time, and some people are simply here to teach us a lesson."

The above saying has helped me make sense of many different situations in my life. Times I have struggled to understand why people come and go from my life. Sometimes this process has hurt quite deeply. It's this quote that allowed me to find peace with it.

People have a great deal to teach through our interactions with them. One massive lesson I learnt was accepting people for who they choose to be. Not to see them as the person I wanted them to be or who I thought they *could* be. Instead, to make my opinion based on who I observed them *choosing* to be. This lesson was delivered through various people in different situations, each lesson building on the next to create a greater overall understanding.

One part of this lesson came from someone I considered at the time to be my best friend. I shared everything with her. All the things you only tell someone you trust wholeheartedly. But, whilst sitting around at dinner with mutual friends, she began openly sharing some of my embarrassing stories without permission. I was hurt and shocked. To make matters worse, she was sharing with gossipy friends you wouldn't tell much to. At this point in my personal growth, I had not yet accepted all of my past, and here it was on public display. Trust was instantly broken.

As time passed, I tried to move on and forgive her. Instead seeking gratitude for the relationship. But the underhanded comments didn't stop. We were in the same friendship circles, and there were times she would interrupt conversations with others to share more of my embarrassing moments. She would jump in to tell stories about how I got drunk one time and the antics that followed. Each time it was crushing. Not only because it was embarrassing. It was like I wasn't allowed to leave my past behind me.

At that point, I didn't see my past as my strength. Rather, it felt like an anchor trying to drag me down, to keep me small and to stop me dreaming. In time, I knew the relationship wouldn't be healed, and I let go of the connection. She was going to be whoever she chose to be. I didn't have to agree with her choices, and she also didn't have to change. The lesson here was to accept people at face value. We are all changing and growing at different rates, sometimes in different directions. I have a huge amount of admiration for what she achieves in business. She is exceptionally brave and doesn't hold back. Something I could learn from and step into more. **The gift in finding acceptance is the freedom and the healthy boundaries you develop. These give you gentle control over how you interact with people in your life.**

Throughout the years, I have met wonderful friends who have become so precious to me. I have learnt who my core group of friends are, which is exceptionally small. I also have a wider group that nourishes different aspects of myself. In general, they are all learning, growing, and reaching for their own set of goals. There is such a different vibe hanging out with people who are on a journey rather than accepting the status quo. The conversation is different and more inspiring, and it's natural to lift one another up and throw ideas around to solve problems. It is true what they say—when you are neck-deep in your problem, you usually can't see the solution. This is when talking about problems and asking thought provoking questions can be beneficial. It creates a space for new possibilities and solutions to be discussed and uncovered.

I am not one for conversations designed to complain about something just for the sake of complaining. To me, this is a waste of oxygen and everyone's time. There are greater things in this world than complaining about something or someone.

Often, when complaining about people and situations, you do so with people of similar values and beliefs. This is because it gives you the validation you're seeking. With no one to challenge your thinking or behaviour, and everyone going 'uh-huh, yes, oh my gosh, they didn't', you find yourself sitting firmly in an ego state. In this moment, the ego is seeking familiarity to prove that you're correct to feel hard done by. When I find myself in a group conversation set around complaining, I welcome the interjection of someone with another point of view which will challenge me, my ego and the group to see greater possibility. Everyone benefits. Ironically, this behaviour is usually not approved of by the group because it is a reflection on an area for growth for each one of them. Ouch.

If you are being the voice of reason, just ensure your ego isn't driving the direction of your point of view. Ensure your mind is open enough to possibly be wrong. As soon as you put yourself on a pedestal, in this instance, you have lost humility.

As far as complaining goes, there are times when venting is required. Not everyone needs to hear you vent, though. Keep that for close friends who will let you get it off your chest. Comment, 'That bitch!' and then you all move on. No need to dwell at the bottom of the barrel. Everyone has good days and bad days. How could you differentiate a good or even a great day if you only ever had one type of day? The bad days help you to appreciate the good ones, and the good days help to appreciate the great days. It all comes back to gratitude and appreciation for everything, even the bad things.

When it comes to friendship, you shouldn't have to prove yourself. It should flow with ease and grace. If you believe you need to prove yourself beyond being your authentic self, this could be a sign that you are yet to find your people. It's important to recognise when it's time for something to come to an end. There is a tendency to try and fight to keep hold of things and people. Personally, I can still be guilty of this. What is important to realise is that letting go doesn't necessarily mean an end per se. It just means that the reason the person is in your life has changed. **From friends to acquaintances, or acquaintances to friends, your relationships will constantly move and adjust as you grow.** I cover this topic of letting go more in a coming chapter.

I have noticed during my personal growth journey that the people in my life have reflected my next lessons and areas for growth. This is called mirroring. **Relationships have an uncanny ability to be your greatest mirror.** People are wonderful mirrors. You can discover the worst in yourself by what you see and want to complain about in others. If you have an intimate partner, they are generally one of your biggest mirrors. When you argue, you are virtually arguing with yourself, except the other person has a different life experience, therefore point of view. How often do you both find yourselves saying, 'Well, you do that too,' or something to that effect? I giggle when I think about the arguments I had with my ex-husband, when it was obvious we were both guilty of the same thing. This is the beauty of the mirror—once you can recognise the behaviour in yourself, you can overcome the problem. Solving it at its root cause. There is a catch, though. It is not always advisable to point out the same behaviour in the other person. This can be frustrating because it requires you to be the bigger person and not necessarily ask them to change. This is the art of *acceptance*.

What generally happens is that the other person will recognise the change you are making and will therefore—hopefully—reciprocate. In time, if this doesn't happen, you have full rights to point the behaviour out, especially if it truly is something that requires change for the relationship to flourish. The situation will generally correct itself without the need for additional confrontation. If you make the changes yourself without putting expectation on the other party, trust the rest will fall into place.

You can also use the mirror to identify where you may need to grow personally. When it comes to using the mirror as a way of self-assessment, first take note of what the person is doing that annoys you. Then ask yourself the following questions: Do I do this also? What would be the purpose of doing this? Why would I do it also?

Your ego will want to say hell no, simply because it wants you to think that you are better than the other person. You will generally find that you do the same annoying thing in one way, shape or form. Now you have the awareness of your behaviour, you have the choice to change it. Ultimately, this decision may change how you interact within that relationship. It is your ego that will keep you at arm's length from experiencing so much more love and connection with yourself and others. The ability to have this really does come from a place of knowing you are worthy of receiving all the love and acceptance you are seeking, and not beyond giving it to another. It all begins with self-awareness and acceptance of yourself and others. Equal giving and receiving of energy.

This universe in which we reside is one of polarity. As you learn and grow, the concept of equal giving and receiving comes more and more into play in relationships. We all know someone who takes and takes and takes. Eventually you recognise it, get the shits with it, and start to say no. This is the start of personal development. This comes from creating a standard for how you want to be treated and how you treat others. In time, these standards become boundaries. You don't allow people to treat you less than you deserve.

The other side of giving and receiving is asking for help. I used to find this almost impossible to do. I would push myself until I was near death before I asked for assistance. Why? Because I considered it a weakness. Ironically, when I was a people pleaser, I never viewed those asking for help as weak. It was only weakness if *I* were to ask. This belief was one I had gained from my mum. Bless her cotton socks, she is a strong and resilient woman. No matter what was thrown at her—my abusive dad, financial strain, horrible people—she always stood with her head held high. This is one of those areas in which I am deeply grateful for my mum. For showing me resilience. She demonstrated that no matter what happens, you can always find a way through. But she rarely asked for help. So being the human meaning-making machine, and with how highly I regarded Mum as a strong, resilient and self-reliant woman, I took on the belief that asking for help was weak. Ultimately, it came at a high cost. I struggled to ask for help, even when I needed it most.

For me, it has been a journey of discovering balance in giving and receiving. I have learnt balance is not always available. With all things in life, there is a time to push and a time to pull. Growing taller as a child is almost like rebelling against gravity, as a tree does, or a flower, even water vapour. We push against gravity's pull. The world is always moving and shifting, nothing is ever stagnant for long. One thing I have embraced when it comes to personal development is the concept of being a lifelong learner. Albert Einstein is quoted as saying, "Once you stop learning, you start dying." And it's true. Like a seed, your potential is unlimited. Who knows what you will turn into? You might be a pumpkin seed. Or you might be a sunflower who has the capacity to turn to face the sun all day long. Either way, you were never designed to remain a seed. **There is nothing wrong with you that does not allow you to grow into exactly what you're meant to be. You just need to determine what direction you wish to go and begin learning and growing in that direction.**

Care for yourself and absorb the nutrients of a full life, complete with love, fun, laughter. People will come and go. No matter how long they choose to stay and whatever lessons they teach you, embrace each one. Love completely and unconditionally. Unconditional love is learnt through self-love first and completely accepting yourself. Then you will understand how to give unconditional love to others.

People are here to teach you lessons. And you are here to teach others lessons. I can guarantee that if you live life to the fullest and don't let fear get in your way, you will live the most extraordinary life. Face every moment of fear head-on. Flip it into excitement. Dream big. See each choice as a step forward on this adventure called life. And at the end of the day, if your legacy was to bring joy, love and laughter to those who entered your life, then it was a life worth living and a wonderful thing to be remembered for.

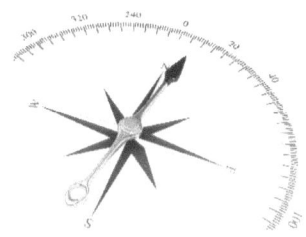

7 - Intimate Relationships

As a basic need, a man needs to feel significant. A woman wants to feel heard.

Although I haven't had the best track record when it comes to relationships, what I did learn through sixteen years in one and the separation that followed is that it takes both of you to make it or break it.

If each person takes ownership of the quality of the relationship, you have two people independently working towards improving and bringing the relationship together. When the quality of the relationship is on one person, you lose balance, and resentment is likely to grow.

Intimate relationships also provide a playground to explore new beliefs and boundaries. The people closest to you will be the first subjected to your changes in behaviour as you put these boundaries and beliefs to the test. You will make demands based on what you require, whether it's time, money or support. Usually, these demands are made with chests puffed up, from atop an egotistical high horse. You will be more difficult for the person you love most because you believe they accept you and all your imperfections unconditionally.

The trust to feel safe enough to demonstrate this behaviour in such a raw form is gained over the years the relationship is built. With friends, you are likely to talk about how you're going to do something. Your intimate relationship sees you put it into action. Vulnerability is at an all-time high. You're on high alert for any danger. Like a deer in headlights, you become highly sensitive, especially to criticism. This is where communication is key. Talk to your partner about what you are looking to change or create. Tell them about the old beliefs that are coming up for you. When they are better informed, they are better placed to support you in your journey. A positive life partner will be supportive. Maybe a little daunted, but still supportive.

When it comes to newer relationships, they often teach us different lessons. New relationships do not have the benefit of time and can therefore lack the same level of trust and commitment. When I first jumped back into the dating scene after my husband left, I learnt lots about myself. I noticed I was quickly becoming clingy and needy. I was telling myself that I didn't need a man, yet I didn't feel whole without one. In general, I was happy, but my insecurities about wanting to love and my fear of not being loved again were creating neediness for a guy. I was wanting them to make me feel more significant, loved, and ultimately worthy—something that should come from within. In acknowledging this, I took my power back, and I worked on developing more self-love. I no longer sought out a man to fill a perceived gap. I could learn to love myself completely. And for all those other situations, I had my trusty vibrator.

Having the desire to change is absolutely key to changing the outcomes in your life. Without willingness to change, you are not going to do what is necessary to obtain the levels of awareness about yourself that will ultimately lead to the freedom of self you truly desire. To escape the dark Cave, you need to be willing to venture into the deep, dark areas of your soul you have been too afraid to venture into and open those cans of worms which are holding you captive. You need to let all that crap out in a way that is safe and productive for you to get where you are wanting to go. At times, you also need to be prepared for everything to fall apart so it can be put back together in a whole new way.

For a relationship to work long term, both individuals need to be growing, with space given for that growth to occur. It is about understanding what your partner requires, being grateful for them and what they add to your life, and not making them the source of your happiness. Do things for one another that build on and deepen intimacy and connection.

Intimate relationships can also contain a lot of conditioning based on the environment you grew up in. We have all heard the saying that men marry their mothers. And ladies are no different. We tend to seek someone like our fathers, or the polar opposite if your upbringing was less than perfect. Either way, the person you seek will have traits based on your beliefs. Now, I know you're saying, 'I don't consciously make the decision to find the same type of person.' That's because it's all happening on a subconscious level. If you're single and keep finding you attract the same type of person, maybe it has something to do with your beliefs. It's a good idea to look at and understand your beliefs around the opposite sex.

As a side note, gender roles are determined by beliefs. If both men and women can do anything, is it naturally the women's role to be caregivers, or would you be happy about a man taking on this role? Biologically, females are conditioned to prefer a man who is more dominant or a good provider. In other words, 'dominance' can be seen as a masculine energy. Feminine energy is naturally gentler and more nurturing. Both sexes have feminine and masculine energy.

A woman who has been single for a long period of time will need to be shown she is safe to release control in order to step into her feminine energy. If the male doesn't allow her to feel safe and as though things will be taken care of, it is unlikely she will relax and step back. This can lead to complications in the relationship because the male may not feel needed or significant.

To understand your beliefs and expectations around relationships, start by completing the statements below:

A man/woman should be ....

A man/woman should always ....

A man/woman should never ....

A relationship is ....

A relationship isn't ....

I expect a partner to be ....

I am worthy of love because ....

I am not worthy of love because ....

I deserve happiness because ....

I do not deserve happiness because ....

Write down everything that comes up for each statement, then look again at your answers and determine whether the statement is actually true for you.

Once you are clear on your beliefs around relationships, it's time to challenge those beliefs. Ask yourself, 'Is that what I truly want for myself or from the person in my life?' Once you are clear on what you want in a partner, you will be able to make a much more informed decision about your relationship and the direction in which you would like to go to achieve the life you are ultimately seeking.

This doesn't give you permission to just walk away because your current partner isn't doing what you want. This is an opportunity to open the conversation and determine what the other would also like from the relationship. **Communication, compromise, commitment, trust and love will pull any relationship through problems.** Every day, it should be a choice to be with the other person, not a requirement.

It's also important not to lose yourself in a relationship. Just because you have a ring on your finger, or have made some other type of commitment, doesn't have to mean you give up you. You should never have to give up on or change yourself for another person. They should complement you, and you should complement them. Neither should feel as if they must sacrifice themself or their dreams for the other person. It is about supporting one another to grow and reach your ultimate potential both individually and collectively. This may pull some people apart, but it also has the power to create an incredibly strong connection.

Relationships are a dance. They aren't all sunshine and rainbows. They're hard to keep strong and require daily doses of love and attention to improve them. It is too easy to become complacent, especially when you have been with the same person for a long time. This is one of the things I learnt through my marriage falling apart. As much as he may not have been willing to grow, there were insecurities of mine I wasn't looking at. This meant I wasn't growing within the relationship. I didn't do little things that made me feel sexy and desirable, which over time changed the way I felt about myself. There was more we both could have done to grow the relationship. We just chose not to.

8 - Letting Go of People with Love

The process of letting people go is one that weaves throughout your life. I have had many people come and go. I found the process of letting some people go easier than others, and much of that is to do with the impact they had on my life. There are times when you don't want to let go, but it's what's required to honour your growth. Family has fallen into this category for me.

I have experienced many moments where I would think myself lucky to never again have to deal with the drama which surrounds my family. There are also moments when I consider whether I would regret my choices if they were to pass away. When making difficult decisions on whether people stay or go, never make the decision when you are angry. Instead, allow the emotions to flow. Then chose what will bring peace to your heart, mind and soul. Those who bring chaos are often teaching a lesson.

When contemplating the place someone has in your life, start by having no expectation of them. I have found this is most beneficial.

They are allowed to live their life, as you are. It's unconditional acceptance of them and the life they want to live. It is the same unconditional acceptance you want *from* them. Acceptance and speaking your truth mean gaining greater access to your personal power and not operating from your ego.

The ability to speak your truth comes through trial and error. You won't get it right every time. There are times when your best intentions are misconstrued. Not everyone is going to like you or what you have to say. You don't like everyone; everyone doesn't need to like you. If you believe you need to be liked by everyone, ask yourself why. It will often be linked with people pleasing, which is covered later in the book.

Developing acceptance for yourself and others is a wonderful gift which aligns beautifully with forgiveness and gratitude. There is a difference between having acceptance and being *in* acceptance. Having acceptance is more of a thought process. It's the acceptance of the behaviour but not necessarily the person. It's more like having tolerance. Being in complete acceptance combines acknowledgement with forgiveness of the person and the behaviour. **To accept only the behaviour means you're still judging the person. This is not true acceptance.** It is like saying you're showing unconditional love for a child when you only give them positive attention if they're doing what you want. The depth of your acceptance will ultimately be determined by the love and acceptance you have for yourself. That is the uncomfortable truth. Being and giving anything comes from authenticity and not needing to prove anything. Needing to prove something is your ego. Avoid the ego in this instance or learn from it. In doing so, you will live an authentic life.

In the times when acceptance alone doesn't assist in finding peace within a connection, this is when letting go may be required.

There are many different reasons you will consider when deciding whether someone will remain or go from your life, and no one can really tell you what to do in these situations. Only you can make the decision which is best for you. Trust yourself and your intuition. Allow this to guide you in your decision making. Personally, my family has had its share of issues which left their scars. Each of us has chosen to heal in our own way to a depth we have individually decided. There is no right or wrong in this, just acceptance. Things do not always work out the way you hope. Understanding you do not have to be subject to the chaos is showing yourself love because you are caring for your mental state.

Letting people go tends to hurt everyone involved. It's not an easy decision to make and has the potential to teach you a lot. Sometimes, it is helpful to know that if they are meant to be in your life they will find their way back. But don't hold out for that occurring. You need to let go of the expectation that it will happen. By holding on, you are putting your life on hold and not truly letting go. By letting go, you may be unknowingly teaching the other person a lesson, encouraging growth. That alone is an incredible gift to give someone, even though it can hurt at first.

The separation from my husband gave me the opportunity to use all the tools I had developed over the years of discovering myself. It reflected all the insecurities, pains, fears, and everything else I thought I'd outgrown. I also developed new ones.

Separation broke me. I began to deny everything I had worked so hard over the years to become. This one decision from another person made me question whether it was all worth it, whether I was worthy of achieving my goals, and whether it would ever happen. I would be lying if I didn't admit that I considered suicide during the first few months. I allowed myself to believe the separation was my fault, due to the emotional rollercoaster I put my ex through while healing from the pain of my past. He told me that my goals and aspirations were taking too much of my time. There was one point during an argument when he referred to the process of my growth as emotional abuse towards him. He had been my pillar of strength, and it crumbled from the weight of that burden. Stubbornness literally kept me stepping up to the plate again and again. Taking on each day and lesson.

From my new vantage point, I see what an incredible gift my ex gave me by being brave enough to end it. In many ways, I am grateful because of the person I am now and the even greater possibilities which are now available in my life. There have been many silver linings from his decision. I have conditioned myself to find the good in every situation. I was never going to remain broken, sad, and angry. I will always find the gold which hides behind the pain. Forgiveness and healing allow for this. From there, I move forward.

Letting go and being let go of allows space for so much change, no matter which end of the stick you are on. You need to look at your insecurities around self-worth and self-love and aim to change that narrative. The funny thing is that as soon as I made a commitment to focus on me and simply be open to receiving what was meant for me, everything started to show up. It was then my choice as to whether to take each opportunity or wait for a different one. You don't always have to take what shows up first; you have choice in life. Again, follow your inner guidance or connect with higher guidance if you are so inclined. In doing so, you will receive the answers you seek. Allow yourself the space to heal, to gain the most from the situation.

Letting go can be selfless, and it can be selfish. I try not to judge it one way or another. When you're acting authentically, without ego, and from a place of love—even when it is self-love—you cannot go wrong. Combine that with trusting your intuitive guidance, and you have a winning combination. You will learn an important lesson, be a part in teaching one, or maybe both will be true. Ultimately, it will give you more of you. In the end, only you can answer the question as to whether someone stays or goes. Just be sure to ask yourself whether you are willing to own the outcome and the lesson of the decision.

Always remember to pick up your lesson when you hit the ground. After all, perhaps it is the reason you hit the ground in the first place—to lead you in the direction of your life path. Every lesson has led me to the next stepping stone. Sometimes it's another fall, and other times, an exciting new opportunity. You must be open to receiving both. To have everything in life means being open to receiving the good and the bad. You cannot choose just the good because it is more comfortable. It will limit your life considerably. You do not grow when you're comfortable. Embrace the dark to gain greater access to your light.

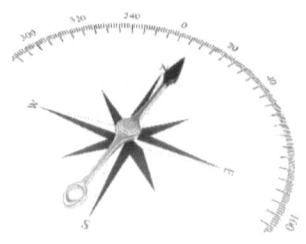

9 - Be Unpopular

How much greatness has been lost by the desire to fit in? Think Einstein: he looked like a nutty professor and was known to be socially awkward, but his ideas and scientific discoveries were groundbreaking. Throughout history, people with a different point of view have been ridiculed, made an example of, and even killed. Imagine how Galileo was treated when he proposed that the world and all the other planets revolved around the Sun. He was forced to recant and put on house arrest until he died for his "blasphemy". Jesus was crucified for saying God was above the Roman Emperor. History shows so many examples of those who had a different perspective, and as a result, created incredible change in their lifetimes. They dared to look at the world differently, and we have all benefitted greatly from it. Nothing incredible was ever created from the desire to follow the crowd and fit in. So, I dare you to be different and be the outward expression of your true self. Share your authenticity with the world. You are incredible, and maybe the difference you bring is what the world actually requires.

We have explored how relationships can be mirrors for growth. Now I would like to delve a little deeper into how you can be a mirror of growth for others. When you stand authentically in your truth, you can reflect back to people what they may not have accepted or acknowledged about themselves. Humans often choose to move away from what is making them uncomfortable. This tends to be an unconscious decision. Generally, it is those with the wildest of dreams and ideas who can truly make an impact on the world, simply because they do not see the same limitations as the majority. Where many see uncertainty, they see opportunity. Where many see fear, they see excitement.

I sometimes wonder how many people I rub the wrong way simply by being happy. It is amazing to me that when you're happy most of the time, people automatically assume there is something wrong with you, or that you have some good drugs. The irony is that so many people are chasing this very thing yet struggle to recognise it when it is right in front of their face. The automatic response is to judge and criticise it because it's unfamiliar. Those suffering from happiness can usually see the reason these people have not yet gained access to joy. It's usually due to a lack of healing. They are still holding onto old stories, pains and beliefs which are not serving them in creating the life they want.

I have had this exact scenario within a work environment. It was probably about three months into the job that the underhanded comments started. My coworker would question why I was so happy, adding, 'It's like you are throwing it in people's faces.' It had taken a lot of internal work to find this happiness. I had learnt to love and appreciate all of me, even the quirks and dark side of myself. I wasn't going to let someone make me feel less than just because I rubbed them the wrong way. When you're authentic, happy and joyful, you become a magnet, attracting the people who appreciate who you are. You find your tribe. Yes, others won't like you. Your light will illuminate their shadows. People tend to play it safe when it comes to being socially acceptable because, in the moment, it's easier than being judged.

Healing is painful. This is why people don't choose to do it. Who in their right mind would openly seek to sit in painful emotions? Yet this is exactly what is required to gain access to lasting, authentic, lovable joy. It is the joy you get to experience from learning to truly love yourself. Every painful situation you have experienced is a brick, and you carry those everywhere you go in life. Every time you heal, you remove a brick from your shoulders. Some traumas are much larger bricks. Over time as you heal, you become lighter. No longer weighed down by the bricks of life. The lighter you feel, the higher you fly and the more joy you have access to. Don't discard the bricks.

Use those bricks to build a new empowering home for yourself. **Each brick is a lesson learnt. The bricks are helping you build your home of wisdom.**

As you repurpose your emotional bricks, it isn't uncommon for this to lead to the dropping of physical weight. During the first nine months of my separation, I lost a considerable amount of weight. I cannot tell you a figure because I don't know, but it was approximately two dress sizes. For full disclosure, I drank a vast amount of wine, but I also created great habits around exercise to aid with stress. Running and other forms of cardio workouts assisted with the weight loss, but that was not the aim. It gave me something to get out of bed for every morning and put me in a better headspace. The positive changes in my body came as an awesome side effect. Losing all this weight ultimately brought new friends and caused others to step away.

People will always judge you, positively or negatively, no matter what you choose. This is why you should allow your authenticity to guide how you want to show up in the world. You must be willing to step out of your comfort zone in the areas where you're trying to remain part of the crowd. Embrace who you are authentically, not who you think you should be. It is about being seen unapologetically in your authenticity and not dimming your light to make others comfortable. This means being seen inside out.

Being unpopular means you are doing and being something that many are unwilling to do and be. You can judge yourself for it, or you can embrace it and be a little more daring to step into all that you are. The more unpopular you are brave enough to be, the more you will be unfaltering in your authenticity. And that is truly beautiful in so many ways. Others will always judge, so just choose what is going to make *you* happy for the long term.

By being authentically you, you're being an invitation for others to be authentically themselves also. Don't play games; you will end up regretting them as you grow older. Life is meant to be lived right now, in this very moment, with as much joy as possible. Don't let the opinions of others limit your life. Expand beyond them. Be unpopular enough to lead the way rather than follow the crowds and the breadcrumbs of life. Sing to your own tune and dance to your own song. This is how life is truly meant to be lived. Those who are meant to join you will always find you because they will be singing their own version of the same song.

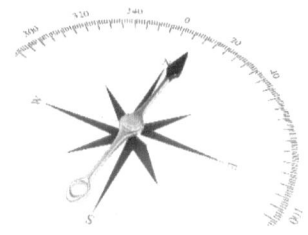

10 - Program Your Brain for Success

"The greater the gift we consider our lives to be, the greater the quality of our lives." - Kylee

Throughout life, you develop stories about yourself from experiences and situations you were exposed to. These stories can define your life in a way that holds you back from the life and success you truly desire and want to achieve. They can limit your thinking of what is possible, therefore limiting the possibilities in your life.

When was the last time you allowed yourself to dream big? And I mean *big*.

If there were nothing to hold you back from what you truly desired, and you had all the time, money and support that you needed, would you go for it? For some of you, the answer would be, 'Hell yes!!!' Yet for the vast majority, even if the first response was yes, you would soon start to get that sinking feeling in the pit of your stomach and retract back into your shell, pulling back any inspired thoughts. It could be a negative or 'realistic' thought, such as telling yourself you can't do it. You then shove everything back inside, including your hopes and dreams. The walls go up and you decide that life as it currently stands isn't too bad.

So, what causes this sudden shift? It's uncertainty and fear rolled into one. You pull all your energy back towards you and pretty much suck it into your body, reducing who you are to the size of your body. The outward energy was your hopes and dreams. Pulling all that back in reduces it to ideas without action. The need to do this comes from the ego trying to keep you safe and predictable.

The ego does a wonderful job of keeping you safe. It lets you know that you're about to step into unchartered waters and, with no evidence of success in this area, it reminds you that you're much safer to stay with what you know. BORING, but at the time it feels like reasonable advice. To grow and achieve wonderful things, you need to be in the habit of pushing the boundaries of your ego and expanding your world. By expanding your world you can be, do and have more. Drive that energy outwards. There will be times when you will get it right, and there will be times when you will get it wrong. It's all about celebrating the wins and the times you learnt.

Imagine if you created a list of all the possible ways to achieve something with the intention to test each one to see what did and didn't work. You could strategically work your way through the list, put a green dot next to the options that worked, and put a line through the ones that didn't work. This process is the same for life, although we don't tend to make the list. The only list we seem to keep is the list labelled "failures". The ego keeps it as evidence of why you shouldn't try something new. Failures are simply options that didn't work. When you learn, don't beat yourself up about it. **Allow yourself the opportunity to get things wrong. Failure is part of life. Accept it and move on.**

Also get into the habit of celebrating smaller wins. There is no reason why celebrating an achievement that came easy is not as important as celebrating the big wins. Humans seem to love this idea of struggling, but what if you didn't have to? What if life came to you with ease, joy and glory as standard, and struggle was foreign? Hard work is still necessary, it just doesn't have to feel like a struggle.

The greatest challenge you will face in trying something new will be yourself. The way you think will determine so much of how you experience the world. The more you push past your comfort zones, the more malleable your brain becomes. It allows you to see the world in a different way. The technical term for this is neuroplasticity—your brain's ability to develop new pathways and reprogram itself.

Every morning, you wake with new neurological connections, and you get to choose what to do with them. Therefore, creating positive change starts the moment you begin to wake. If you wake up every morning dreading the day, then this is the emotional state you continue to live every day, until you decide to change it. Instead, choose to remind yourself of how lucky you are to be alive and how magical the world is. Use affirmations upon waking to remind yourself of what you want and who you want to be. Remember to state them in present tense. An example of a present-tense affirmation is: 'I control the direction I am heading in my life.' This states an outcome you are seeking in the positive—how you want it to be—as if you already have it, in present tense. It's this combination that tricks your brain into believing you already have what you are seeking. As part of the process, address any of the negative or limiting beliefs you have which are contrary to the affirmation. I will discuss how to do this later in this chapter. Additionally, affirmations tend to be quick and easy to remember. It is also important to remember that saying it once or even ten times is not sufficient; you need to repeat this affirmation daily as often as you remember, as if you are living it, until you *are* living it.

A limiting belief is a belief you hold that doesn't support you in a more expanded life. In other words, it keeps you stuck where you are by limiting what you believe is possible. Most of your beliefs are determined by age seven. If you aren't actively making yourself aware of your beliefs, then you are potentially living your life from the perspective of your seven-year-old self. This is why you will come across adults who react to situations like children. It's because they haven't challenged the beliefs and behaviours they learnt when just a child. Take for example a child who is given everything they want. When they don't receive something, they have a tantrum, yelling, stamping their feet and exclaiming how unfair it is. I have seen way too many adults who still have tantrums like this.

Assisting people to challenge their beliefs can be so much fun. You will see the person become increasingly agitated as who they have believed themselves to be shifts. This is where my willingness to be a catalyst for change and hold space for the individual becomes important. Holding this space can be very uncomfortable. People only tend to make change once they are very uncomfortable with their current situation. Sometimes, this means making people aware of what they are doing and asking them why they continue to do it. It's about asking the uncomfortable questions to make them uncomfortable enough to embrace change. It also provides the clarity required to understand why that change is required. It could be the thing that frees them from a lifetime of living Groundhog Day and allows them to finally begin to experience life in a new, expansive way.

The reality is that change can be, and generally is, uncomfortable. To acknowledge that you haven't had the best default programs—beliefs—to operate from can be challenging. Noticing where a belief and its linked behaviours have created crap situations in your life can be a hard pill to swallow. I know, I have swallowed a lot of them. The benefit of the tears, growth, and ultimately self-forgiveness is that you have a new platform on which to build the rest of your life. You begin to build a new foundation. We hear from people in their 50s and 60s that they wish they had learnt these types of lessons earlier in life, how different their lives would have been. This is the gift that I have recognised I've benefited from personally. Doing all this "work" has allowed me to step into greater and greater versions of myself that ultimately created the person I am today. I know my journey hasn't ended yet and it won't until the day I die. There will always be more areas for me to grow into, and challenges which will allow that growth.

I often joke with those who do my online programs that they will probably want to kill me. They will discover things about themselves and the world that they can't unknow. Once your eyes are open, it's a choice to shut them again. Once you have acknowledged how something has held you back, you are then never able to turn back and knowingly make the same choice again without understanding the repercussions. Sometimes, I just wished I could unlearn it.

However, I also didn't want to go backwards, so I just had to suck it up, change and move forward.

So, how do beliefs actually shape your life? Great question, and I am glad you asked it. This is important to understand in order to put all of what has just been discussed into context. Beliefs are truths that you just know. These are as varying and individual as each person on this earth. Two people will rarely share the same belief and have it mean the same thing. Some examples of beliefs would be, 'I am great at swimming', 'people enjoy spending time with me', 'I am funny and light-hearted', 'I enjoy challenging my body with new exercises'. Beliefs are the filter in which your brain sorts out the information coming in from the world around you. It takes in 10 million+ pieces of information each second and determines whether something is important enough to bring to your conscious attention. This is one reason why police obtain several different witness statements. Each witness has seen the incident though their own filter and will therefore see it slightly differently or notice different pieces of the puzzle. To demonstrate this further, I would love for you to do the following exercise.

Exercise

I want you to imagine you are standing on the corner of two busy city streets. Make a mental note of all the things you see.

Some of you will see in your mind a still picture or image. For others, you may imagine a movie playing through your mind. Neither is better than the other, it is simply an inbuilt preference. What is important is the picture or movie you have imagined is what your brain, through experience, has determined is relevant. The movement of cars, the colours of lights and the people who could get in your way would form the basis of what you saw. Now put yourself back on the same corner you just imagined. I now want you to notice all the sounds you can hear both near and far. Maybe there are birds chirping from a park nearby, or as they fly by. Maybe people are chatting, engines idling and revving up as they take off, there are crosswalk signals beeping, you hear some horns off in the distance, there are high heels clicking on the pavement. These are just some of the noises you may notice. Now I want you to feel. I want you to feel the warm breeze as it blows down the street, someone knocks into your left shoulder and apologises as they pass you. You notice how the breeze moves your clothing. Notice the feeling of your clothing brushing your body, your hair moving in the wind. I also want you to notice how the ground feels beneath your feet and how your feet feel in your shoes. Are they comfortable? I want you to feel your feet wriggle in the confines of the shoe as the weight of your body moves and adjusts over each toe. Now feel the beating of your heart and the movement of your breath as your chest rises and falls. With all those experiences in your mind, I want you to notice how bright the sun is. What colour are the traffic lights now? What colours are you and everyone around you wearing? What colour is the road? What colour are the lines on the road? What are the colours of every vehicle, and what does each individual driver look like?

I can imagine given all these descriptions that you may be feeling relaxed right now, or possibly stressed. At every millisecond of every day, your brain is bombarded with all this information from the sights, sounds, smells, and feelings occurring at every moment. This is why your brain filters and categorises information. It is why you can find yourself on autopilot driving and when you arrive at your destination, wonder how on earth you got there. It is your brain's ability to decipher all this information at rapid speed that allows you to function at the most basic level. There is no way you would be able to achieve anything if you had to consciously notice every little thing that was happening at every moment of the day. You would become stressed, and it would be harder to identify danger.

It is also this filtering process that allows you have lightning-fast reflexes. Your brain has the capacity to notice something as soon as it seems out of place and focus your attention in that direction. If you do not consider guns to be dangerous, seeing someone walking down the street carrying one may not even cause you to notice them. On the other hand, someone who sees them to be dangerous will likely notice it very quickly. Your beliefs determine everything you do and don't consciously notice. This means you will only notice that which is previously determined as important, unless you make a conscious effort to notice different things. Opportunity or threat? Important or irrelevant? Your beliefs are deciding for you.

The brain is very quick to judge. It takes conscious effort to consider things completely. It was interesting to notice that after my ex-husband left, I met men who were very attentive and did things that I would have had to beg my ex for, such as just watching a movie with me. Ironically, I was more comfortable with the guys who would virtually ignore me afterwards or be less willing to communicate between catchups than those who were attentive and message and call me regularly. The more supportive they were, the scarier they were because they were less familiar, and their actions didn't match the story I was telling myself. My belief that I wasn't worthy of being loved completely. This is where self-sabotage began. I knew that I was worthy of having it all, yet what that looked like was very unfamiliar and therefore very uncomfortable. This generally isn't the feeling you are seeking when looking at whether someone is going to be a part of your life or not. *Wonderful, you make me feel uncomfortable and I question your every act of affection; let's hang out.*

There was one person in particular who I was overthinking way too much. I was trying to pinpoint why and what was making my stomach twist in knots when I could see where he would be a great partner for me. Why did I want to run? I started to think maybe it was because I didn't feel safe. It wasn't until I recognised that who he was and what he had to offer me in my life was simply unfamiliar, that I could allow myself to relax more and enjoy the process of getting to know him. If I didn't have the awareness around my sabotaging behaviours, there is a huge chance I would have screwed it up and chosen to be with someone more comfortable. When you have big dreams, you need someone who has the capacity to support you, push you, and encourage you forward. They also need to have the self-confidence and awareness that your dreams don't take anything away from who *they* are and want to be.

Beliefs Exercise

Neuroplasticity plays a huge part in your life and how you experience the world. Your beliefs reaffirm what you believe and therefore what you notice as important. Knowing you can use neuroplasticity to create the life you want gives you the power to change anything. Therefore, having the capacity to identify beliefs and utilise your neuroplasticity is key to being able to recognise and ultimately challenge the ones that are holding you back. Changing your beliefs can literally change every facet of your life. To change them, you need to know what you are looking for and how to overcome them.

Keep in mind, finding one belief can link to another one on the same topic. So, as you notice them, write them down along with everything that comes to mind because it will all be very beneficial in understanding what the belief means to you. Is it supporting you or bringing you down? Your writing will seem very sporadic, with random words to describe yourself or an emotion. This is exactly what you want. To provide an example, you may write a belief in relation to your body such as, 'I am ugly' followed by, 'fat, unlovable, gross, no one loves me, not worthy'. These following descriptive words are all the stories you are telling yourself as to why you hold that belief. You will have one or multiple events in your life that allow you to hold onto those descriptions and therefore the belief. Look at each of these stories, then reverse the negative belief by positively affirming what you want it to be. The example here may be, 'My health and fitness improve every day, and I can see the positive changes in my body.' Don't overlook the story because this is the glue that keeps the belief in place. The key is to come to peace or acceptance with what occurred, so you can forgive, let it go with love, and move forward. This is where you will truly be free of the belief and will begin to live the affirmation of your goal life or desired outcome.

Let's start uncovering your beliefs. I want you to consider the types of beliefs you have around your money and finances, relationships, health and fitness, work or business, self-worth, and so on. You are looking to uncover the beliefs you hold about yourself and what you are capable of being, having, or achieving. If you are unsure where to start and what to look for, start with statements that begin with the following. Write as many answers as you can for each of the statements:

I am..

I can..

I can't...

I always...

I never...

People should...

This activity should get the thought juices flowing. If you are truly committed to changing your life, grab a blank piece of paper and do the work. Become aware of your beliefs and thoughts and challenge the hell out of them. If you're telling yourself that you can't do or have something, why can't you? Or is it just an excuse to not live a full life? If you are truly committed to yourself, would that answer change? That is the key to challenge the beliefs you hold and being okay with the uncomfortable answers.

There are more areas you can venture into, but this will potentially open a big enough can of worms to start with. Know that you are not expected to overcome every belief in an instant. Coaches who know Neuro-linguistic Programming (NLP) have an effective tool and process they can use to assist you in overcoming beliefs. In saying this, as much as the conditioning may be gone, your continued awareness around the belief will assist in removing any conditioning hiding on a deeper level. Changing these beliefs will alter your day-to-day behaviours and therefore life.

It is important to be aware that beliefs are directly linked to behaviours. As your brain seeks evidence of them, your behaviours are driven by them. You act in accordance with your beliefs. If you think someone does or doesn't like you, your behaviour towards them will differ based on which belief you hold. So, if you find yourself wondering why you do something in a particular way, it is most likely linked to a belief somewhere.

Beliefs form the structure of who you are, so understand that this process alone will cause you to grow significantly, should you do the exercise. It will challenge all the beliefs that are not allowing your world to expand into greater possibility. Do not limit yourself in any way. Any limitation is just a belief hidden somewhere wanting to keep you playing a small game. Where there is a desire to be or create something greater, there is a way to achieve it no matter your circumstances. Don't allow small thinking to limit the life which is truly possible. Step into fear and uncertainty and see where the journey takes you. You never know what is around the corner until you get there. Embrace the journey every step of the way. It will lead you to something greater.

11 - Create a Vision

One of the best things you could do for yourself is to create a vision for your life. Personally, the vision and desire to assist others was the only reason I was able to drag myself out of the deepest holes during dark times in my life. **With all that I knew and taught to others, I was still not immune from those deep moments of doubt, fear and depression.** In those moments, there was so much uncertainty. Especially during my separation.

Certainty is a funny thing. When it's all gone, it's what you crave. The desire or need to know what is around the corner can be exceptionally strong. But you will never know until you arrive. It doesn't matter who you ask or how else you delay the arrival. You will only find out once you use courage to venture there despite the uncertainty. Build up the courage to walk up and look around the corner. Follow that idea or passion to see where it goes.

I have learnt many different things from different business ideas, including my network marketing endeavours. Ultimately, I fell upon the creation of my own business so I could chase something that had a greater purpose for me on a soul level. As much as people bag out network marketing, I believe it can work. But it is not easy. It is bloody hard work, especially in the beginning. You need to become accustomed to judgement and being rejected again and again and again. Those who succeed should be celebrated because they have had to do a shitload of personal development to be able to make it in the industry. Think about it. As much as everyone loves Tupperware® and its lifetime warranty, no one wants to go to a party. It is the conundrum of multi-level marketing (MLM). The products are usually fantastic, but people don't like the mode of delivery. Strange, given its usually friends sharing the product.

Whether you like or dislike MLM, it is one type of business model. More importantly, those who keep at it are doing so for a reason. They have created a vision for *why* they are doing it. Generally, this is referred to as finding your 'why'. It is basically the deepest reason as to why you're doing something. This can be applied to why you want to start running, start a business or any other goal you are working towards. It is this 'why' or strong vision which is going to push you through the hard times, through the judgment and all the setbacks. No matter what you are trying to achieve, setbacks are a guarantee. It's your ability to handle these setbacks that will either put you ahead of or behind the pack. This 'why' can pull you from your darkest moments, if only to give you a glimpse of what you're longing for.

When my ex left, he told me my dreams were taking too much of my time. He also said he didn't want to be a part of where my vision was taking me. I guess I should have taken it as a compliment that he believed I would get there. Either way, my goals and vision were enough for him to know he didn't want the same things as me. My moment on the bathroom floor thinking about my big vision also came with the thought that it cost me my marriage, and was it all really worth it?

I thought of the movie *The Devil Wears Prada*, when Meryl Streep says to her young counterpart that when your life falls apart is when you know you have made it. This was that moment of possibility that made me get off the floor, wipe the still-flowing tears off my face and take my drunk ass for a walk to clear my head. That evening was the darkest moment of my separation. The vision of what I wanted to create seemed impossible. I had no idea how anything was going to work. My part-time job wouldn't be enough to provide the kids or me our basic needs. The rug was well and truly pulled from underneath me, and I had no idea where to start. I felt like nothing short of a total failure, and a rejected one at that. I didn't think that my children would want to be around me. I considered that I could simply set them up with my percentage from the separation going into an account for them to access when they were much older. In that moment, it felt like my entire thirty-three years on this planet had either been fighting for myself or fighting for others, and I was exhausted.

At that point, my business was growing. But it was nothing close to a success. After years of working to make it happen, learning, changing things, selling items of mine to finance it. It was not yet successful in the terms with which I defined success. That reality check was a tough pill to swallow. At the same time, I knew that nothing would show up how I expected. I always had the thought and hope that success was always just around the corner. I just needed to keep moving forward, and eventually I would find that magic connection. In the end it was my vision of lifting others so they could find hope and purpose in their lives that pulled me forward. My separation was just another experience I could use to have greater compassion and understanding for my clients.

Life has taught me to be a fighter, even when I didn't think I had the strength to fight. I have always managed to find a small ounce of strength to pull me through. Sometimes it was the smallest of things, like a movie quote, which had the power to make all the difference. **There is one thing that I am certain of when it comes to getting through hard times, and that is having a strong vision gives you the power to pull yourself through anything.** Add that vision to wanting to create something that serves others, and you have a winning combination. You're not only doing it for yourself but for the greater good as well.

When my life crumbled, I put my business on hold to get a stable financial foundation for my kids, and I worked my ass off. I saved everything I could. I furthered my studies and aimed to be an active member in the community. I set myself goals and took steps every day to achieve them, and I did achieve them. Three years is what it took to achieve those initial goals, which even included a two-week camping holiday for which I needed to buy all the gear and car to get us there. I left with very little and built up everything else from scratch.

So how do you go about creating a vision? Well, there are lots of different ways based on what you are wanting to create. An important thing to note is that your vision doesn't have a be big. No one is expecting you to go out and create world peace. On the other hand, if this is what you are working towards then I will cheer you on all the way. The most important thing is that it resonates with you, and it is something *you* really want. When I quit smoking the first five or so times, I was doing it for my ex-husband. The time I succeeded was after much pleading from my eldest daughter. She said she didn't want me to die, and neither did I. Having lost Dad and Omah to cancer, it was a real risk. The fact that I was smoking quadrupled my risk. I didn't want to die when my kids were still young. I wanted to be there so that one day I could be a grandmother myself. It was this desire that kept me going strong, and I have remained a non-smoker. I honestly cannot see myself falling back into that now very expensive habit. I know that quitting smoking doesn't guarantee I will see life to the age where my children will have kids. Maybe they won't want kids at all. Either way, I know I have now given myself the opportunity to live a hopefully long, happy, healthy life.

Exercise – Your Ideal Average Day

If I were to ask you to create a day in your mind that you could live every day of your life, what would it look like? I don't want you to create a day of being on holiday, lazing on a beach drinking pina coladas. As unlikely as it may feel right now, you would eventually tire of this life and begin to seek more purpose. Create a day where you are serving the greater good and doing what lights you up. It needs to be specific. What time do you wake up? What is the first thing that you do upon waking? Where do you live? Where is it situated? Who are you spending your time with? Which friends are around you? What would you eat? What freedoms are available to you? What are you doing to earn income? All these things put together will create your ideal average day. There will be approximately ten years between creating this concept, taking consistent action, and achieving it. The bigger the dream life, the bigger the action that is required. What is important to know is that anything is possible if you believe in yourself enough to create it.

These days, my vision pulls me out of my darkest holes and keeps me from the deepest corners of my Cave. It is **seeing myself on a stage talking to hundreds of people about my life and how to truly live a life of joy.** Travelling from state-to-state delivering seminars, running group workshops for people who want to delve deeper into their individual situations, running and facilitating events and getaways. To truly have a positive impact not only on adults but children and teens as well. There are so many things I wish I knew when I was younger that had the potential to change some of my decisions. It is those things I want to teach. Maybe through my pain I can inspire someone to see the potential in themselves. From where I sit right now, I have no idea how this is all going to fall into place. What I do trust in is that if I keep following my path through all the twists and turns, eventually I will find my way. When that moment happens, my breath will hitch in my throat as I realise I am living that moment. It will be then that I may truly acknowledge myself for the contribution I have made to the greater good and helping others find the light in their lives.

With big goals, it's also easy to lose sight of where you're headed.

It hides just over the horizon and cannot yet be touched, just felt in your heart and seen in your mind. This is why it's important to celebrate and acknowledge the smaller wins. At one stage, where you are right now was one of your goals. Whether it is the house you are in or having saved enough money to get your hair cut. Every day you're ticking off your to do list, and every day you achieve more than you realise. It is only through allowing yourself to acknowledge these things that you truly see how far you've come. Each day may look like the one before, but when you look back twelve months from now, you will see how much has changed. You will see how far you've come. **Life is always shifting, moving and adjusting. Each small step taken every day compounds to create massive change.**

I know when you're feeling low it's difficult to create a large vision, so my recommendation is *don't*. Start small, almost too easy, something that you know that you can achieve, and when you do, celebrate it. Celebrate like it was a huge thing. Give yourself a high five or a pat on the back or any other gift to acknowledge the achievement. This is about building the evidence to support the belief that you can do whatever you are looking to achieve. Know it is still a step in a new direction. That direction can be forward, left or right, just not backwards. Life can sometimes make you take a step back, but don't do it on purpose. The only time you should go backwards is when you're looking to see how far you've come and to acknowledge the things you have learnt along the way.

As you achieve more and more, you will feel yourself reach further towards the light at the entrance of your Cave. You will know when you're ready to start upping the game with your goals. You will test the levels of your potential with longer-term goals and ones that will really stretch you. Norman Vincent Peale, author of *The Power of Positive Thinking*, said, "Shoot for the Moon. Even if you miss, you'll land among the stars." If you have a big enough goal, there is a chance you may not achieve it, but what an incredible journey you will have trying to get there.

In the end, if I don't have my moment on that big stage with the hitch in my breath, I will be happy with knowing I have followed the guidance I have been given in the best way I understood it. I can ask no more of myself or of my angels who guide me. I am thankful to them for always being by my side and carrying me through my low and dark moments. I feel so blessed with the talents I have been given in this lifetime to work with people for the greater good. Ultimately, the person I have become as part of this journey is so much more rewarding than I ever could have imagined. I am so incredibly grateful for myself and the choices I have made that have created who I am in this very moment.

Life will always be uncertain. The more you try to control it, the more you lose control of it. The greatest gift you can give yourself is to allow what happens to happen, and trust that it is happening for your greatest good. I remember hearing this so many times when I was younger; that God never gives you anything that you can't handle. As uplifting as this is, I never really understood it 'til I had discovered more of who I was and had some 'if only I knew this then' hindsight moments. There are times when you will be challenged to the point where you will wonder if you'll be able to keep going, and times when it seems you have no control over what is happening in your life. It is in these moments we need to remember you are always perfectly placed on your journey. If you were meant to be somewhere else, that is where you would be. It is this sense of having a purpose and a path that can help you find the light in your Cave. **Your life is not wasted. You are simply learning what you need to learn for your next step in life.** Put simply, you're on your way to where you are meant to be. Simply trust and go with the flow, following those quiet callings from deep inside your heart even when they don't seem to make sense.

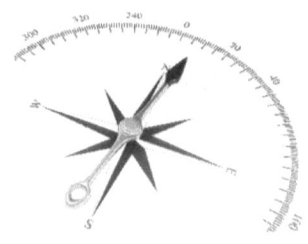

12 - Manifesting and Goals

With any vision comes the requirement of setting goals. If you are committed to achieving your vision, you can consider that to be the big picture goal. When you have a big goal, the key is to break it down into smaller bite-sized pieces. This is so it feels a little less overwhelming. These smaller more achievable goals will be the stepping stones on your journey towards your vision.

When you have a goal that is set in the distant future, say ten years or so from now, be open to how you get there. I can guarantee it won't show up at all how you imagine it would. The road forward isn't straight. If I look at my life, for example, I never could have predicted the big shakeups that came. Instead, you just need to grab your surfboard and ride the wave as best you can. If you're like me, you will fall off more than a few times and get back on to ride the next wave. Embrace the twists and turns in the path as best you can and try not to lose faith or focus.

When there is a long road to travel, remaining focused can be challenging, especially during those twists and turns. There are different ways to keep focused. One such way is the use of a vision board. If you're creative and have a few spare hours on your hands and a bunch of old magazines, this can be a useful tool to keep your eye on the prize. The science behind it is that you are constantly reminding yourself of where you are heading with visual cues. This gives your brain something to search for as you move through your day. You'll be more likely to take the inspired action in the direction of the goal.

The use of the right images, words and other relevant visual cues will train your brain to recognise important opportunities in the world around you. For example, have you ever seen a car and thought, 'Wow, that is a nice car. I would like to have one of those.' Then once you buy one, everyone seems to have one, and you start to notice them everywhere. This is your brain in action. You send out an electrical charge directed at an item. Your brain notices the chemical changes in your body at the thought and the respective emotions which follow. To feel that more often, your brain will remember and direct your attention to what created that reaction, which in this example is the car. This is what many call "deliberate creation". It forms part of the Law of Attraction.

When I first heard about the law of attraction, it seemed like spiritual mumbo jumbo. Still, the idea was intriguing enough to kick off my personal development journey and ultimately lead me to where I am today. You may not want to believe in angels and spirits, but the Law of Attraction is backed by science. It's as real as gravity. Like attracts like.

We are like radio transmitters at every moment of the day, and these energetic waves, or vibrations/frequencies, can be recorded and gauged with fancy instruments. Everything in this universe, even outside of this planet, has a particular vibration. Flowers, trees, money, other people, the list goes on. Both living and non-living things have a vibration. Science tells us that everything is 99.99 percent made up of the space between atoms. There is only a small portion of anything that is solid. Even a brick wall is mostly space. The biggest difference between that and, say, water is how the particles are arranged. The way particles are arranged gives things their properties and shape. Does this mean that everything is not as we may have perceived it to be? Very possibly. Maybe we do live in a world more like the Matrix. Instead of being unplugged, maybe we learn something interesting that allows us to wake up to what is truly possible in this world.

When it comes to aligning with vibrations, the quality of your thoughts and feelings plays a big part in your ability to adjust your vibration. The process of meditation allows you to quiet and focus the mind. It also provides mental space in which to explore your dreams and desires as if they have already happened. Aligning your vibration. Because of this meditation can be an amazing tool in assisting you to 'quicken' the process of bringing the future you desire to you. Although, as I shared earlier, don't be like me and simply try to *think* things into reality. This isn't quite how this process works. There are things you need to do. This process of deliberate creation is referred to as "manifestation". The interesting thing about this process is that once you begin to understand the absolute power of the human mind, some of the stories of what is possible will blow you away. It is all those unexplainable chance encounters of being at the right place at the right time, and so much more. I don't believe in coincidence. To me, these instances are signs that are guiding you, or they're an indication that you are on the right path. They are aligning to create what you desire. Sometimes the opportunities which present themselves require you to step up, even when you're not sure you're ready. Maybe this is divine guidance or a combination. You may never know. It is in these situations you can lean on faith.

Every minute of every day, you are creating. Research was conducted by the University of Western Sydney in relation to exercise and the power of the mind. Let's say the exercise was running. They compared two groups: one group did the exercise with the aim of reaching a particular fitness outcome, and the other group just watched videos and visualised themselves doing the activity. Those watching the activity had recorded increases in heart rate, respiration and skin blood flow as a result. Meaning minor gains were obtained. Does this mean you can watch videos of people running then go run a marathon? Well, maybe not, but it does make you wonder whether it is possible to get a little fitter from the couch. The reason the people who didn't physically do the exercise still benefited from watching the video is because **the brain is unable to determine the difference between doing an activity and visualising it.** I know myself, when I have been watching something physical on TV such as a fight scene in a movie, I will feel my body stiffen. Different muscles will activate as I also dodge the punches. This is this experiment in action.

Your brain has much greater capacities than science completely understands. We only know a small amount about the brain and what it can do. Maybe we will never know its full capacity. To learn more about how amazing the brain is, I recommend reading a book called *Switch On Your Brain* by Dr Caroline Leaf. I remember riding my bike for hours listening to this book. Most of the time my mouth was open at the huge potential of the brain and how little of it we use. Understanding the brain opens such a huge amount of potential, even into how you react to situations. It's basically Life Coaching or Psychology 101. **Your cognitions play a huge part in how you live**

your life and whether you will achieve your goals. If you say you can, you can; if you say you can't, you can't. To break it down, no matter what you are telling yourself, you are correct. So you might as well make it a good story and one that takes you in the direction of your goals and dreams.

I saw this firsthand whilst teaching my kids to rollerblade. My youngest daughter took a little longer to get used to them and, at first, was being quite hard on herself. She was telling herself and me that she couldn't do it as she fell again and again. I kept reminding her that she could and that if she was going to keep telling herself she couldn't do it, I might as well sell her skates as she would end up being correct. I held onto her to provide some confidence and reminded her to believe in herself. I reminded her she was just learning and that it was normal to fall over. The confidence started to grow, and before long, she was off on her own, claiming that she was on her way to being a pro. I wasn't about to crush her dreams, so I told her to go get 'em and have fun. When you're telling yourself you can't do something, this belief changes the way you behave. In the instance where my daughter was telling herself she couldn't rollerblade, she wasn't holding her body upright. She was like a floppy doll. As her confidence grew and the belief was challenged, she started to believe in herself, hold herself up, and ultimately skate on her own.

Understanding cognitions gives you the understanding and knowledge to challenge your thoughts and beliefs and change them to assist you to move forward. If you consider your cognitions to be the cogs of your brain, how they turn determines how you will experience your life. Your cognitions are basically made up of your beliefs and your beliefs drive what you see and experience in the world. Consider the example of seeing a particular car everywhere again. In this example you changed your cognition to say, 'Hey, this car is important and desirable.' So, your brain goes to work to ensure you are notified whenever you see one.

Your brain will see everything before you are consciously aware of it. **It is your brain's job to filter, file and coordinate all the information flooding in at every moment of the day.** Think back to the street corner exercise. This is where the conscious and unconscious parts of the brain come into play. The conscious brain is what you likely notice the most; it's the thoughts that you are aware of. The deliberate actions, if you like. Your subconscious brain does most of the work sorting through the information coming in to determining what is relevant for you / your conscious brain to be aware of. The subconscious brain is how you can drive home and not be sure how you got there. You don't remember doing the steps to get from A to B. The subconscious is the powerhouse where your dreams become reality. This is because it is where all the information is kept in relation to your beliefs and past experiences and traumas. The subconscious uses this information to determine what is filtered through to the conscious part of the brain. In the radio frequency analogy, you could say it is a key component to the antenna. If you are interested in reading more about manifesting and the brain, Dr Joe Dispenza is your main man. He is the link between science and spirituality on this topic.

The process of manifesting is the aligning of your thoughts and emotions to create seamless transition. To explain simply, it is to live as if you already have what you are seeking. **Your subconscious radio transmitter can bring forth what you are looking to create.** Remember, your brain doesn't know the difference between real and imagined.

I read a book called *You Already Know* by Helen Jacobs. It suggests that manifestation occurs once you have healed emotionally in the areas that are impacted by what you are looking to create. This made a whole lot of sense once I had grown and healed through the majority of serious events in my life. Everything shows up quicker and better than I could ever plan for myself. The biggest key I can suggest is don't limit how something can show up. Put the ask out there then get on with your life with joy. Don't judge or try to predict how it should show up. Asking for the "what" rather than the "how" allows for a lot more magic and possibility. It usually turns out better than you could have imagined yourself. It is the process of healing, holding positive expectation, and trusting in the process that will ultimately create the life you're seeking. The moment you're in the energy of lacking or wanting, it pushes what you're desiring away from you. Your internal story is saying you don't have it. So, that is what you create: more of not having it.

Holding positive expectation and a positive emotional state when you don't have what you are seeking can be challenging. Often, it is when you reach the point of giving up and moving on with your life that it suddenly appears. This is the level of non-attachment you need to maintain to manifest your desire. What is also important to mention is divine timing will also play a part. It won't show up until the right time and, unfortunately, you do not get to determine when that time is. When it does fall into place, you'll understand why it didn't occur any sooner.

So, dream big. Go wild. Heal from negative beliefs and change your emotional state. Set the goals then take inspired action towards your desired life. You can achieve it. Anything can truly be possible.

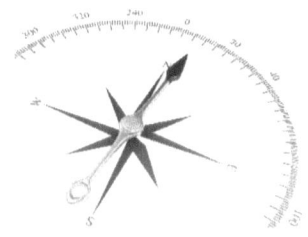

13 - Setting and Achieving Your Goals

The purpose of this book is to help you acknowledge yourself and learn how to step into greater versions of yourself. One way in to do this is through setting and achieving goals.

If you have previously done work in relation to goal setting, you may have heard about the concepts of **S.M.A.R.T.** (Specific, Measurable, Achievable, Relevant, Timely) goals. This acts as a guideline to writing or outlining your goals to increase the likelihood of success. It also allows you to think about ways in which to measure your goal to ensure you stay on track. It ensures you're not setting yourself up for failure by creating a goal that is not actually achievable. It looks at your priorities to ensure they support you as you work towards your goal. This will also assist in reducing distractions and excuses that will show up from time to time.

When it comes to achieving goals, limiting beliefs are not the only thing that will hold you back. Failing to consider what is important in your life—your priorities—will also determine whether you will succeed in achieving any goal. There is no point saying you're going to go to the gym five days a week when logistically you don't have the time. As much as time can simply be an excuse, we need to be mindful of starting at an *achievable* level and building up. Remember the stepping stones. You are more likely to achieve success if you make a small change then build on that in a way which keeps you moving forward. Start by going to the gym three days a week and aim to build up.

When it comes to weight loss, so often people have a short-term view. They aim for temporary pain, such as eating no chocolate, sugar, or bread for a certain period then go straight back to their old habits once they reach that goal. Before they know it, they're back to where they started and unhappy. Look to the long term, as in your entire life. Or are you wanting to diet and sacrifice continuously throughout your life? When you take this long-term approach, it becomes about changing habits that you can stick with and become part of who you are. Looking at weight loss specifically, when did skinny become more important than healthy? Learning to eat in a balanced way that supports your nutritional requirements and goals should be the aim. Healthy habits will give you everything you desire for the long term. It may just take a little longer to get there.

As we discussed in the last chapter, you must have a good enough reason why you want to achieve a goal. Without it, you may find it difficult to find the pull to get you through the hard times. To do this, you need to become really clear on *why* you want it. Sometimes you need to make that reason bigger than yourself. If you have kids, your "why" could be to do it with them and demonstrate what healthy living really is. The things you do and involve the kids in will work towards creating their values, beliefs and adult behaviours. When it comes to health, I just want to point out that your emotional health is even more important than choosing a carrot over cookie, and your emotions are heavily determined by your mindset.

The mindset you carry into achieving your goals is incredibly important. Your emotional health forms the foundation on which the actions towards your goals are built. Imagine if achieving your goals was easy and enjoyable. So often you dread changes to your life because you immediately begin to look at all the things you have decided you won't be able to have or do anymore, like chocolate. Already you are stepping into the victim mindset and a state of lack. Is this the foundation you want to achieve your goals? Questionable at best. This is why looking at our mindset in the beginning, prior to acting, is so important. Set yourself up for success and plan first. In general life, I really don't like planning things, I prefer spontaneous moments. This is because much of my life is structured with minimal wiggle room for last-minute decisions. Structuring my day is about setting myself up for success in as many areas of life as possible. Between kids, appointments, life, days can be pretty busy, and it can be easy to forget things. My calendar is my saviour, and just one way I schedule my day to ensure I maximise the time I have available and fit in my priorities.

When shifting your priorities, the moment you find yourself thinking about the things you will no longer have due to working towards a goal, you need to pull your head back into line. Remind yourself of why you wanted the outcome in the first place. A 'lack' mindset will 100 percent sabotage your success. It's not about what will be missing, it's about what's being gained. Remember your big "why". Get clear on whether this is a lifestyle change or a temporary fix. I encourage you to always look to the long term as this will assist you in creating the most.

Setting and achieving goals are also highly beneficial from a growth perspective. The important thing about goals is not just in setting and achieving them. It's the person you become in the pursuit of them and the things you learn about yourself along the way. Whether that is about making and keeping a commitment to yourself or something different, these are the things that make all the difference in your life and provide wonderful building blocks for developing greater versions of yourself. Goals are not just goals when you begin to understand how they impact your growth.

The achievement and commitment to pursuing your goals will

ultimately end up as evidence that you are worthy, enough, lovable, belonging and so much more. During the pursuit of your goals, you will change your beliefs about yourself. Chasing goals will give you direct access to your beliefs around your "triad of self"—self-worth, self-love, self-respect—which I will discuss later in this book. It is through this triad of self that you will build a strong foundation. You develop the evidence your brain can use to challenge and overcome any limiting beliefs. These beliefs form the core of who you are, so it is imperative you look at them to reach greater and greater versions of yourself. It is through overcoming these beliefs that you will be drawn out of your Cave and stand with the sun beaming on your face.

Working towards achieving goals is not about perfection, it is about aiming to be one percent better than yesterday. You will get some things wrong. Expect it. Just don't give up because of it.

Goals are a great tool you can use to achieve the things you want to create in your life. They are the bridge from where you are to where you want to be. This is why the foundation needs to be solid. Some bridges have trolls or wooden planks missing. This is the reason your "why" needs to be so strong—to get you through those challenges. Every goal you set, you're making a commitment to yourself. Know that this commitment has a direct link to your self-worth, and failing to take the required action only means you are adding to your Cave. For your sake, ensure your commitment and that you are able to achieve a goal before you set it. Really think about it, but don't let limited thinking be the reason why you don't go after it. Remember to start small. You are better off having a whole list of smaller goals ultimately taking you in the direction of your larger goals than you are having one big goal and no idea how to get there. Taking this approach of having a series of smaller goals will give you a greater sense of ongoing achievement.

Be open to how some goals show up. Some of my goals I have achieved by accident. It was simply through the process of being happy and having that as my aim that the rest followed. Set your goal, just don't forget to enjoy the journey. Life is supposed to be fun. When things are no longer fun, you don't want to do them anymore. Keep your goals acting like an arrow or compass in life, keeping you on track. Don't let them take over your life. Let them be a contribution to where you are headed but not your reason for existence.

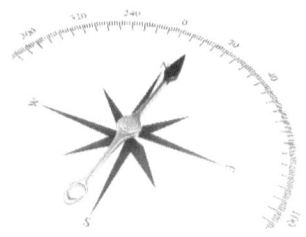

14 - Habits

The daily habits you develop impact the outcomes in your life. It is the accumulative effect of time that makes this happen. Time compounds your actions to take you in a particular direction. The benefit of this means it doesn't matter how small a step you take towards your goals. If you continue to take those small steps every day you will achieve your desired outcome. The smaller the steps may mean it will take you longer than someone who is running, but either way, you will also reach your destination.

To make that small daily step, all you need to aim for is to be one percent better than yesterday. It really doesn't matter what your goal is, the principal of aiming to be one percent better will always apply. Elite athletes are always looking for that one small thing that will take them above their competition, that one thing that will give them the edge. In the book *The Slight Edge*, Jeff Olson writes of an elite cycling team investigating the quality of sleep being achieved by their athletes. The team's managers changed everyone's mattresses to ensure a high quality of sleep and therefore recovery. For us mere mortals, as much as the quality of our sleep is important, our one percent is likely to be something more directly linked to our goal. Using the example of exercise, it may mean being active every day or meeting the veggie consumption recommendations for the day. Also keep in mind that each day you add something new, it doesn't replace the previous day's one percent activity. You are looking to continue adding things and removing the things you notice are not working. Aim to constantly test, assess, and adjust your thoughts and actions as necessary.

Whether you believe it or not, the quality of your thoughts is a habit. We have all come across someone who is eternally negative and seems to suck the life right out of us. This is a prime example of someone being in the habit of negative thought. Changing negative thought patterns can take a little while to work through. You must be consistent. Although, this is not a reason to delay making progress towards your goals. Remember, one percent better every day, no leaps or bounds required. The reason negative thought patterns can take some time to work through is because they are likely connected to a belief. So, until you uncover and deal directly with the belief, the negative thought pattern will likely continue. This means you need to become acutely aware of what you are thinking and when.

Keeping a thought journal can help with tracking your thoughts, although it can be a time-consuming practice depending on how you do it. Some people do this as part of a morning or evening journaling practice. Implementing this could be your first one percent. Others will keep track of thoughts throughout the day. Like a food journal for thoughts.

No matter how you track or become consciously aware of your thoughts, it is a necessary process to change your life. To become aware of what your triggers are and where your limiting beliefs may be holding you back. Mental roadblocks tend to show up a few weeks or months into your journey to success. These thoughts will be linked to your self-worth and will highlight the areas in which you don't believe you are worthy of the outcome. So many programs are ninety days, yet it's the weeks after that test your commitment.

The further you have set your sights, and I encourage you to be daring, the more stepping stones you will have along the way. For example, when I was training to hopefully win my category in a one-hundred-kilometre mountain bike race, I set a goal of a minimum number of kilometres I needed to ride each week to build my fitness and stamina. There was also the need to change my mindset from disliking hills to telling myself the quicker I rode up them, the sooner I would have it over and done with. So, I encouraged myself to dig deep on every hill. I experienced many instances on the bike when I learnt that the body continues long after the mind starts and ultimately stops complaining. There have been times when I could no longer feel my legs, yet they continued to spin as if by magic. When you push yourself to your physical limits, sometimes you just need to keep going until the mind gives up. In these moments, you free yourself of the mind's limitations. In other words, all the negative thoughts and beliefs telling you to stop and that you cannot do it are silenced.

Every time you step outside of your comfort zone you are challenging the limits of your ego, mind, and commitment to the outcome. Whether it's public speaking or weight loss, self-doubt is likely to raise its ugly head. Every time you notice self-doubt, take it on, Mortal Combat style. Except you win every time. You're challenging the constraints of your comfort levels, taking you to greater and greater levels of self-awareness and success. Rigid walls become a rubber band, and eventually the rubber bands snap, releasing you and your mind from restraint.

Thoughts, values, and beliefs dictate your habits, and your habits determine the actions you take. It all begins with a single thought. To put this into an everyday example, you don't tend to find yourself at the shops and then think, 'Oh, I'm going to go to the shops.' The thought inspires the action. Each thought is proceeded by another. For example, after thinking of going to the shops, you then think about how tired you are or that you can't be bothered, then you calculate how much you really need milk. These following thoughts then determine how driven you are to achieve the initial call to action of going to the shops.

As simple as this example seems, let me expand it into a fitness goal scenario and throw in some negative thought patterns for good measure. Let's say as part of a goal to lose weight, today is your morning pre-work gym session. It's a bit cold out and your bed is so warm. Your initial thought is, 'It's gym day,' which is then followed by, 'It's cold out and warm in bed.' In the first week of working towards your goal, it is likely you were still very inspired and jumping out of bed telling yourself, 'This is it, no more excuses.' Say you are now approaching three months and have made good progress. You begin wondering if missing one session could really hurt. My question to you is what are you going to do? Missing just one gym session isn't going to break all the good work you have done. Or could it?

As much as missing that one gym session isn't going to make you an instant failure, it does lend itself to other issues. It is like an ex-smoker saying, 'Oh, one cigarette can't hurt!' Then they're addicted again. Even after three months, missing that one gym session while this is still a new behaviour could be the start of missing more and more because of the "just one can't hurt" mindset. Be aware there is a difference between it not being possible due to life just going wrong and your *choice* not to go because the bed is warm. From experience, those sessions where you push yourself out of that warm bed mean more for your mental health than you will ever realise. It is proving to yourself that you are worthy and will do what it takes to achieve the outcome. At this early part of the game, it does the most amazing things for your self-worth and self-love. **Every time you go beyond your excuses or your comfort zone, you grow and build trust in yourself.**

Your daily habits will make or break your success in anything you do. Often, it is the small things that make the biggest difference. Again, that accumulative progress of the small, seemingly insignificant things will have you zooming for success. The choice will always be yours based on the demands you make of yourself and how many excuses you are willing to give into. It all starts with a single thought, and those can be changed to programme yourself for success.

Acknowledging that your thoughts, beliefs, and habits may be creating the crappy results in your life can be confronting. But once you overcome them, you become dangerous. You will be unstoppable. No matter what, always step forward and move beyond your comfort zone, excuses, crappy beliefs, and negative thought patterns. Get out of bed!

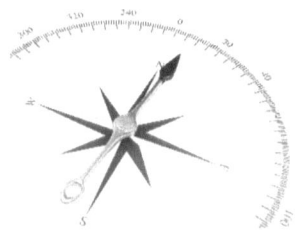

15 - Turning Problems into Possibilities

There are times when problems can really seem to pile up and weigh you down. It's in these moments you can really use gratitude along with other emotional guide points to assist in looking at problems from a different perspective. Abraham Hicks have a wonderful scale in relation to emotions and moving to a better feeling state. It speaks of joy being the number one emotion you want to consistently experience and disempowerment being the lowest emotional state. Therefore to change your emotional state it you only need to move yourself up the scale. I have included the scale below for your reference:

1. Joy / appreciation / empowerment / freedom / love
2. Passion
3. Enthusiasm / eagerness / happiness
4. Positive expectation/belief
5. Optimism

6. Hopefulness
7. Contentment
8. Boredom
9. Pessimism
10. Frustration / irritation / impatience
11. Overwhelm
12. Disappointment
13. Doubt
14. Worry
15. Blame
16. Discouragement
17. Anger
18. Revenge
19. Hatred/Rage
20. Jealousy
21. Insecurity / guilt / unworthiness
22. Fear / grief / desperation / despair / powerlessness

When you change your view of a problem to possibility, you can gain greater insight and clarity. Like a statue, it is impossible to admire all its beauty from just one direction. You must move around it to see it all. When it comes to problems, to be slightly contradictory, it's less about seeing it from all angles. Rather, it's about moving your perspective from one point of view to another, say from being a victim to taking ownership.

Below is a visual representation of these changes in perspective:

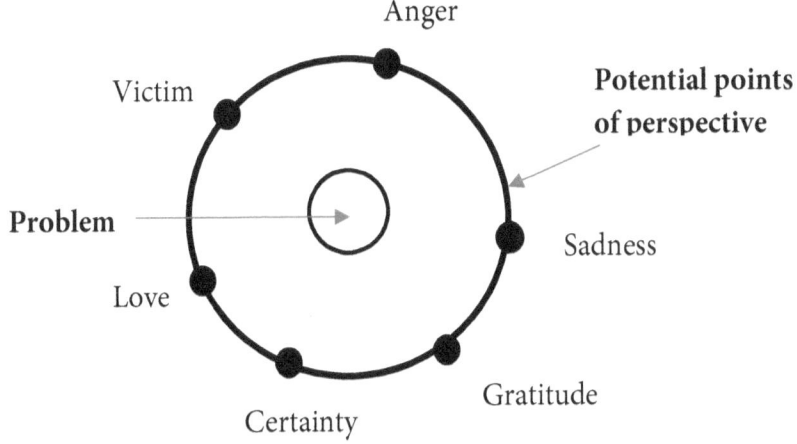

Diagram: Problem vs Potential points of perspective

Please be aware it's only an indication of some of the states of mind from which you can choose to look at a situation. To explain, as a "victim" you're choosing to look at the problem through the lens of "poor me" and blaming others for the problem. The flip side of this is taking complete ownership of the problem and therefore the outcome. From anger, you're still in the victim mindset, just choosing a more aggressive approach. The counter to anger would be acceptance and love. Sadness is where we feel completely helpless, struggling to find potential solutions. The counter to sadness would be happiness and joy, even excitement, in the challenge of finding solutions. Gratitude is where we can change to see the situation from a more thankful perspective. Certainty is the counter to uncertainty, which forms a major emotion when it comes to problems. Often, uncertainty generates fear, which can therefore trigger additional emotions including anger and sadness. Having certainty lends itself to having clarity on a situation or problem. Finally, love is the ability to see the purpose of the problem, to be grateful and see how it was necessary to your personal growth journey.

When you view a problem from the negative perspective, the problem can seem bigger than it truly is. Your mind goes into overdrive with all the potential issues, most of which likely won't occur. What changing your perspective does is provide more options to solve the problem.

This awareness then allows you to choose more analytical thinking, which will assist you in generating better solutions. Alternatively, you can make your decisions based on your emotions, which isn't always ideal. Personally, I use a mixture of the two. Sometimes they are emotion-based decisions. For others, I will weigh up the options available to me and choose the one which moves me closer to my goals.

Generally speaking, when I do this exercise, I aim to lean into gratitude and love for what the situation can potentially create, or for giving me awareness of the things that needed to change. I consider that every situation is designed to teach something, so I am always seeking the purpose behind it. Why have I suddenly injured myself? Does it mean I need to slow down, or is the universe stopping me, so I do what I am supposed to be doing? When things don't go to plan it's easy to step into the victim mentality of, 'Poor me, now I can't do anything because of A, B and C,' but when you expand on the perceived problem, you can suddenly see that *maybe* there was a greater reason for it to occur. **Change can only occur once you have awareness of the issue and its potential solutions.** If nothing is by accident, what is the gift this problem or opportunity can provide? **The key to turning your problems into possibilities is about broadening your perspective, which allows you to see more and more opportunities.**

The longer you stay in the problem, the longer it takes to move forward. I know this seems obvious, so why does it sometimes take forever to decide and take action? It's like those mornings you don't know what you want for breakfast, and an hour later, you're still hungry. The worst part of making decisions is the moment before you commit. Rip off the Band Aid. Just don't be stupid about it. Take a moment to consider what you are trying to achieve and move in the direction of that outcome. Your everyday decisions will ultimately make the biggest difference in how quickly you achieve your goals and dreams.

At the end of each day, what is important is that you live a full life.

You stepped through your challenges and made decisions which supported your goals. Some days you will have more options than others. Others you may need to sleep on for inspiration to strike.

As much as we are all striving towards a greater life, don't lose sight of what is truly important.

Love deeply and fully, experience joy, love yourself completely, and be grateful for those you share your life with. You're blessed to be alive at every given moment. Nothing is guaranteed.

Everything happens for a reason and only at the right time. I cannot help but see every challenge as an opportunity to grow and learn something. The journey will never be a straight line, so don't expect it to be. Life will take you in every possible direction, even backwards, if that is what is required. Turn problems into possibilities. **Every time you flip your perspective, you adjust your beliefs and step towards that which is going to create the most for you.** Life will open a little more. Don't waste the opportunity to truly live. Life is a gift, not a given, and can be taken in a moment.

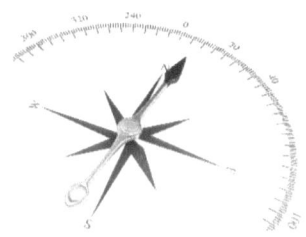

16 - Is it Time to Take Control?

Whenever you make the decision to create change, you need to start by taking ownership over the outcomes in your life. This alone can be incredibly uncomfortable and transformational. When you can find fault in your actions or behaviour in something that isn't your fault, that is ownership. It comes from the awareness that for everything that has showed up in your life, you have had some part to play in its creation. Having read my story, you can imagine that taking absolute ownership of my life had some challenges simply because I had always viewed myself as a victim. Yes, some moments were out of my control, yet my choices as a teenager were very much my own. It was supposed to be everyone else's fault, wasn't it? If you're not taking ownership of situations in your life, you're most likely living your life as a victim. This alone is disempowering you.

Playing the victim is one of the most disempowering things you can do. Through letting go of being the victim, you discover a more empowered version of yourself. It is like a secret superpower. You are not at the mercy of anyone else or an external situation. You have complete control over your behaviour, emotions, thoughts, and therefore what you create in your world. Why am I so bloody cheerful all the time? Well, ninety-nine percent of the time, it's because I made the choice that was who I wanted to be. I was sick and tired of being sad all the time, living on the "poor me" train. I needed to get off that bloody train or I would have killed myself.

I rode the victim train for a very long time. Now it's parked in my Cave, and I am not going to be putting in the maintenance work to get it back up and running. I would be lying if I said there weren't times I have been tempted to hop on. Even though it's a crappy train, the seats are too hard, and you never get to go anywhere exciting. Emotionally, it can feel comfortable. This is because it's *familiar*. It is the ability to see the comparison between who I am now and who I used to be that stops me from grabbing the spanner and hopping aboard.

So why choose to ride this train? Fear and familiarity keep you on the train. It requires a lot of change to truly hop off, affecting friendships, relationships, life, and changing deep-rooted parts of yourself. All these areas feel safe and secure because you know how they operate. By getting off the train, you shake it all up and begin to reevaluate all aspects of self, including beliefs and behaviours. There are also the questions of: if not this, then what, and where is the grass greener?

As you move away from the victim train, you find yourself on the self-love train. The self-love train is always on the move. When you're on the victim train, there is a chance you can't even see it due to your beliefs and a desire to be comfortable. Your focus is on what is going wrong or where you are being wronged. This is due to how your beliefs are adjusting your view of reality. In brief, your beliefs seek evidence of what you believe to be true and disregard anything which doesn't support your current belief structure. Therefore, in this example you would see this fast-paced, exciting self-love train as something to fear due to its unfamiliarity and would therefore avoid it.

You hold the lifetime pass to the victim train behind anger, resentment, fear, sadness, blame, and judgement. This is what the train runs on. The one thing that is comforting about being on the train is you're surrounded with like-minded people. All your fellow victims. It is one big happy family of misery. Everyone makes the most of the uncomfortable seats because they have found friends there. The question you should be asking though is if they are the right people for where you're headed?

Additionally, when you don't know there are more comfortable seats available, you think you already have the best of the best. You don't know what you don't know. I believe this is what is referred to as being "blissfully unaware", but is it really blissful? I discovered this after my marriage ended. I never knew how unhappy I actually was until I experienced the joy of being on my own. I was also able to seek something greater. A love I could only dream of, because I didn't know if it actually existed.

Making the choice to get off the train means letting go of unhealthy connections. The happier you get, the more you reflect to others their shadows. They haven't been prepared to do the work to grow in order to claim their free ticket to the self-love train. You see, the self-love train is the opposite of the victim train. It is going places and creating wonderful things. To truly embrace the self-love train, you must say goodbye to the victim train, its uncomfortable seats, and the people on it—at first, anyway. This is one area I struggled with: the letting go of people and relationships that no longer served me. If you are wanting to create incredible things in your life, it is important to know that you are the average of the five people you hang around the most. At times, I grew at such a rapid rate that the process of meeting people and then outgrowing them was relatively fast.

It's not that you don't appreciate the connections you make along the way. It's more you move in different directions. Only a few will be in your life for a long time, most just for a season. They are on their journey in life, and you are on yours. **Not holding yourself back is showing yourself love.** To hold onto something to make someone else feel better is often doing yourself a disservice because you are not honouring your direction, growth or potential. If you are choosing less, you are accepting the *less*on. Every time I didn't choose growth, it became a lesson. It cost me parts of myself which I had to rebuild to have again. Do this enough, and you realise choosing less is just delaying the process of growth. Therefore, you're accepting to learn the lesson as many times as it takes until it sticks. At which point you don't look back.

As much as I say you simply need to say goodbye to the victim train, it's more of a transition. You may inspire others on the train to also get off. Given that the train isn't moving anywhere, they can make that choice at any time.

Growth never stops. There isn't a magic finish line. You simply gain a deeper understanding. When you are actively working towards what you truly want in life, you begin to feel fulfilled and even joyful more consistently. Then comes a test. Maybe you left some baggage on the victim train, and you miss your friends there too, so you jump back on. It's familiar in its discomfort. You notice how negative the conversations are, how everyone seems stuck in their story and not changing anything to move beyond it. You realise this is not where you want to be, and you miss all the joy and happiness of the self-love train. You grab your baggage, sort through what you want to take with you, and jump back onto the moving train.

Your journey from the victim train to the self-love train will be one of the most thought-provoking, self-awareness growth journeys. You will discover things about yourself that you will most likely not like, but through the acceptance of yourself initially, then the acceptance of others, you will see the true beauty of the journey. Again, this is one of those hindsight things. If you could see the person you were becoming, you'd be jumping off headfirst. But this is not a logical journey. It is one where you align your mind, body and soul. So many people consider this to be a spiritual journey, but it's really a journey to becoming who you were always meant to be. You simply step on the path and choose to lose the conditioning of who you were *told* you were supposed to be.

As I have previously mentioned, I thought personal development was for those who were really screwed up, and I didn't see that as being me. I look back now at that mindset and can't help but laugh. I was completely and utterly screwed up. My thoughts and beliefs were driving my behaviours. The ego, depression and anxiety had such a strong hold on me that I couldn't see what was always in front of my face. That was what I thought life was supposed to be.

Until you dare to leap, you will never know how amazing you are and how incredible life really is. Life truly is a gift.

The longer you stay on the self-love train, the more people you will meet who are headed somewhere. They start to show up, and you develop friendships. Then the self-love train is not so lonely anymore. Life will always challenge you. Being on the self-love train doesn't change that. You don't grow when the going is good. At times, you must become uncomfortable to continue your growth. Just like a flower, if you're not growing, you're dying.

Taking control is all about getting clear on what you want. Set the goals and intentions, grow yourself, make the demand on yourself, the universe and those around you. Take ownership of what shows up in your life. Look at your beliefs. They underlie so much of what you're unhappy with in your life. If something isn't working for you, the likelihood is that there is a belief hidden under the problem. Take ownership and you will overcome it.

17 - Fear

What scares you the most? And I'm not talking about the monster that lives in the closet or under the bed. Do you ever wonder why no matter what you do it's never enough, so you do even more out of fear of not being enough? Do you fear being noticed in the crowd because you feel different from them? Or do you fear being better than someone because they may react unfavourably? Or do you change yourself to fit in with a group out of fear of being rejected and not belonging? These are the most common fears, and they drive behaviour as you try to fit in and not stand out.

While beliefs and fears both impact behaviours, they impact them differently. When I was first starting out as a coach, I would work down through the layers of a problem to determine which fear was the driving force. As much as this generally is one root of the problem, a healthy plant has multiple roots. The beliefs generated from experience are generally the roots feeding the fear.

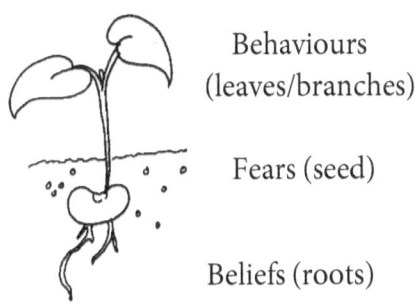

Behaviours (leaves/branches)

Fears (seed)

Beliefs (roots)

Fear will always exist. It comes down to one or a combination of the three main types of fear previously mentioned:

- ∞ The fear of not being good enough,
- ∞ the fear of failure or success, or
- ∞ the fear of not belonging.

These fears are experienced by *everyone*.

Fear is one of those things you can guarantee will always be in your life. To know this is comforting *and* annoying. You cannot grow to the point where you no longer experience fear. So, when fear does show up, why not celebrate it? You are about to step outside of your comfort zone, and this should be exciting. You're about to broaden your scope of reality. Yeah, it will be scary at first and you may get the steps wrong a few times but screw it—live, learn and grow. The beautiful thing about consistently stretching yourself when it comes to fear is that, over time, what once scared you no longer creates fear. When you do it again and again, it becomes comfortable. A kid taking to the field in a sporting match for the first time may be scared, but by doing it every week, the fear diminishes.

Well, until grand final day.

Fear and excitement are experienced the same way physically through the body, it is just the brain that decides which one you're experiencing. So, are you just excited? Maybe fear should be saved for life-threatening experiences, not a run around in a park.

The journey to where you are going is all about who you are becoming and perfect timing. There is no point arriving at the town you are meant to be in before the town has been established. You'll end up looking in another place for what you seek, which is not where you are meant to be. The universe puts roadblocks in your way to slow you down to ensure you arrive in perfect timing. This helps make sense of when things are going well, and you still feel you are making progress, but then something happens which causes you to take two steps back. Possibly, there is something more for you to learn before the next stage is presented. Or maybe the person who you are meant to meet isn't there yet. Maybe you aren't who you need to be yet.

There are so many "what ifs?". The problem with this is that you can spend all day overthinking it. Instead, it may be helpful to change perspective and consider that maybe you are perfectly placed on your journey. If you were meant to be somewhere else, you would be there already. Take the pressure off and enjoy the journey. It is so much more pleasurable if you do.

I have been guilty of pushing my way through life, only to hit more roadblocks. This became frustrating, and I felt a little downtrodden by things not showing up how or when I wanted. Through giving up the expectations and instead focusing on living a purposeful and joyous life, everything changed and rapidly. The key is to expect what you want to show up, but don't stress the details of *how*. Just keep following the fear and the path that will instinctually present itself. Acknowledge that you don't have any control on the how or when and focus on taking aligned actions that move you forward. **Allow yourself to approach life with more ease and joy. From this vantage point life becomes about adventure, purpose and fun.**

I truly believe that all my experiences, especially those that were outside of my control, were preparing me for what I do now and are taking me in the direction of where I am meant to be headed. Without those experiences, I don't believe I would be as driven or have this much passion to make a difference. These events have been my stepping stones. At first, I didn't even know it. Life is always moving you in the right direction. You just need to start noticing the signs and begin to flow with it.

I truly believe when you're ready, the teacher will appear, opening your world even more. You just need to do your part and be open and willing to learn, grow and follow the breadcrumbs leading the way. Don't be a sheep; be the shepherd. Be your own guide, if necessary.

Your goals and dreams are on the other side of fear. It is up to you to chase them. It is up to you to continue to move forward despite the fear. You can reduce your experience of fear by stepping into it again and again until it no longer scares you.

Fear and excitement are experienced the same way, and you can choose which one it is you're experiencing.

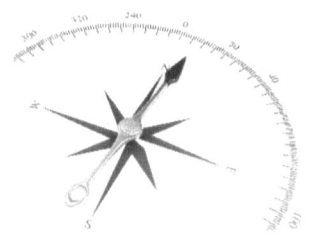

18 - Your Triad of Self

Self-love, self-respect and self-worth are all seeds from the same tree and form what I refer to as the "triad of self". This triad intertwines and flows through all areas of life. To me, the purpose of learning and growing is to step into the best version of yourself every single day. Therefore, anything you commit to and follow through with builds your triad of self by developing self-confidence, self-trust, empowerment and self-love. It assists with keeping the fire in your belly burning bright. The triad forms part of your core self.

You develop it through setting standards and expectations that ultimately become your boundaries. Your boundaries are what you will and won't accept, not only from others, but also from what you expect of yourself. Set these boundaries through trial and error. Even once you have found the sweet spot, you must remember to continue to revisit your boundaries and adjust as circumstances and growth require. Boundaries can be hard to enforce, especially when they're new. You need to be firm in your position and connect with your self-worth. At first, this is done with a good handful of ego to ensure the message is received clearly.

I used to put so much energy into meeting others needs before my own. This is referred to as "people pleasing" and it was destroying my triad of self. A people pleaser is an individual who spends their time ensuring others are happy and cared for before taking care of their own needs, wants and desires. They feel uncomfortable about putting themselves first. They can think of one hundred reasons why their needs should fall to the end of the never-ending to do list. Serving from a full cup is a foreign concept to people pleasers.

The beautiful thing about developing your triad of self and growth in general is that you decide who you want to be and what you want to create for your future. It provides a gap in who you are currently and who you want to be, and what you want to do and have. This comparison will allow you to identify what needs to be done to build the bridge to get you where you want to go. You begin the process by designing and stepping into who you are to become. It doesn't matter where you begin, only that you start.

So, what does this have to do with self-love, self-respect, and in particular, self-worth? Well, everything. It's about knowing that you are more than the labels you, family, friends and society place on you. You can have hopes, goals and dreams, and you're allowed to chase them. An interesting thing I have learnt in working towards goals is that it's not so much about the goal itself—although that is important. It's who you become whilst achieving that goal. It's fair to say that if you were already the person you needed to be to achieve that goal, you would have already achieved it. In saying yes to a goal, you are saying yes to yourself. Your goals will assist in shaping you into the person you are becoming.

The level of self-respect you have for yourself changes your behaviour. Those with high self-respect will make different decisions to those with low self-respect. So many of my decisions, especially regarding my promiscuity as a teen, were born from a lack of self-respect. But I was listening to an audiobook one day and learnt something valuable. Sexual activity is not unusual in girls who didn't have a strong, positive relationship with their fathers. *Ding,* lightbulb moment. I finally had a logical reason why I had treated myself and my body so badly. It all made sense. I was seeking love and attention from males in the wrong way, and from all the wrong people. I simply wanted to be loved. I just didn't understand that at the time.

This is what allocating a better story or meaning to something looks like. In technical terms, it's called "reframing". There may be events in your past that you're not wanting to write home about. Some stories you may never want to pass your lips, and this was the case for me. Discovering the connection between promiscuity and daddy issues gave me the permissions I needed to stop beating myself up. To forgive myself for those crappy decisions. It finally all made sense. I am pretty sure I cried and gave myself a big hug when I processed this along with all the self-hate I had been directing at myself. I was able to let it go. For over ten years, I had carried around this self-hatred. This was all I needed to allow myself to begin to love all of me for the first time in my life. My triad of self increased in all areas. This is the power of information. **If I were to apply a definition to personal development, I would describe it as the accumulation of knowledge that has the power to open you up to different possibilities, and give you access to more of who you truly are. Beautiful, right?**

When I initially set boundaries with my ex-husband around the topic of the kids, it came with a good measure of pushback from him. He had what I deemed to be an unreasonable expectation of me to look after the kids whenever his work or social calendar required.

Given that I was no longer his wife, I didn't believe this was my responsibility. So, the boundary that I set was that when it was my turn to have the kids, I had to sort out care arrangements to meet my schedule, and during his days, care arrangements were his responsibility to figure out without relying on me. In other words, my days were my problem, his days were his problem. Simple. As this didn't work so well for him and his work roster, he had issues. Given the separation was new, my thought was maybe he should have considered that before he decided to end the relationship. High five to the ego-driven mindset.

Either way, having this boundary meant that I was not going to be at his disposal as he desired. There were times this made my life harder. But it was worth the extra work to remove the unreasonable expectation he'd put on me. Changes take time to implement and to become habit. It takes time for yourself and others to accept them. Just don't be afraid to adjust things if they aren't working. This isn't about getting it right the first time. It's about progression, and about putting you and your needs first, hopefully without the ego-driven mindset.

Following through with what you say you will do is another way to improve and build your triad of self. In keeping the commitments you make to yourself, you're demonstrating the value you see in yourself. Through standing up for yourself, you will collect the evidence you need to determine that it is okay to chase what you want. As obvious as this is, the mind pushes against it due to the fears it raises. It fears rejection. Do it anyway. Ask for what you require. If you are not willing to fight or ask for what you want, you risk never achieving it.

I lost track of the number of arguments I had with my ex, the number of nights I walked into a dark room or thought about sleeping on the couch as I worked towards creating my dreams. I began to feel like me and my dreams were a burden, the sound of my typing was too loud and kept him awake, I wasn't spending enough time with him. He told me the kids were suffering in some way from me prioritising myself and what I wanted to create. It took so much self-belief to keep going. It took creative thinking, trying to create a solution that worked for me and them, attempting to find balance. Unfortunately, I never seemed able to achieve that. In the end, I figured no matter what I did, it was never going to be enough. There would always be a greater demand on me, so I prioritised me anyway.

Ironically, I only came to this conclusion once my marriage was over. By this point, I had more time than I knew what to do with to create my dreams and the life I truly desired. Following your heart and doing extraordinary things will not always be easy but will always be worth it. Don't give up just because someone is challenging you or doesn't agree. This is your life to live. Live your life as an invitation to something greater. You have the potential to be the fierce leader you know you can be. Your dreams are valid. Others have the choice as to whether to join you or not.

Chasing your dreams will require sacrifice. You determine what those sacrifices will be. This is one of the major benefits of choice. There are certain things I will not sacrifice for anything if I have the option. Then there are other things I will give away easily. It is all choice. Weigh up the pros and cons and take ownership of every choice you make. Sometimes, I remind myself that short-term pain can lead to long-term gain. If I need to miss out on a few sunny days at the beach to focus on a project and ultimately create more freedom, then that is worth it.

The standards and expectations you set directly determine the quality of your life. If you are happy to have someone dictate what you can and can't do, that is your choice. If you are willing to do the work and build your personal power, you will be better placed to deal with most situations in your life. Be assertive in communicating what you require. Be willing to have the hard conversations and to not sacrifice your goals and dreams. This will mean you are working towards a life that is fulfilling and of your creation. It's about determining what you will and won't accept, and demanding nothing less, then doing what you say you are going to do. By following through with your actions, you're demonstrating you're not full of hot air. That you're serious about what you're wanting to achieve. If you want to lose weight but continue to eat cake and don't do the gym workouts, you're not demonstrating to yourself or anyone else that you are serious about your goal. You're only letting yourself down, and your self-worth will take the hit.

A lack of action is often linked to a lack of self-belief. If you don't believe you can have it, you won't ever do what is required to achieve it. So, if you are looking to change anything, start with overcoming the limiting beliefs you have in that area of your life. Remember, a limiting belief is any thought that tells you why you can't have something. Use the tools previously mentioned to assist you in working through this. Don't use finding these limiting beliefs as an excuse not to start. I can assure you, they will come up soon enough. You just need to be aware enough of your thoughts to catch them.

The triad of self, in a nutshell, is simply a way of being or acting that depicts how you feel about yourself and allow others to treat you. You may find in certain areas of your life you have a higher sense of self than in other areas. For example, at work you may be incredibly confident in your ability to do your job. Therefore, the way you behave and stand up for yourself may be different to how you behave in another area where you feel less confident and in control. When you're still working on creating new beliefs within your triad of self, those who already have a high level of self-worth and respect may come across to you as arrogant. They simply have firm boundaries and standards and expectations of themselves and others, which they are unwilling to modify unless proven not to work or in need of adjustment. This rigidity arrived through trial and error and a deeper knowing of what's required to obtain the results they seek in life. They are committed to themselves and the outcomes they are working towards. A word of warning I would add is, don't be egotistical about it.

Exercise

Try sitting up straight and pulling your shoulders back. Lift your chin and connect to the strength of your empowered self—strong, loved, complete. How does sitting in this posture make you feel?

Still unsure? Sit or stand like someone who is, in your mind, confident in who they are. There has been much research done in relation to how our physiology changes our psychology. Amy Cuddy discovered as much during her research on this topic, and you can easily find her TED Talk on body language online. Amy's research found that when you sit with your shoulders rolled forward or hunched, you tend to experience more of a depressed state. However, if you sit up straight and smile, it completely changes the way you feel. You enter into a more powerful, confident state of being. This outcome was demonstrated again and again in the way the participants felt and acted based on how they physically posed. So, take note of how you are sitting. Are you hunched or sitting tall? Hiding or confident?

When you're living in your Cave, the roof is probably low, so it's no wonder you're hunched, potentially in a depressed state. On the contrary, when you stand in the sunshine and take in that fresh air, you will stand taller with your chin lifted to the sun. Do the exercise, and you may be surprised at how quickly you feel different. Holding either position for two to five minutes a day can have lasting effects, so choose wisely. This is why you will hear some gurus talk about the power pose of standing upright with your legs hip-width apart and your hands on your hips. Stand like this in front of the mirror for a minimum of one minute every day. It may seem silly, but it does work. Before getting on stage, some people will have a special stance or movement they do to connect them to the presence they want to portray on stage. Doing this can assist in removing some of the nerves. In NLP (Neuro Linguistic Programming), this movement or stance is referred to as an "anchor". You set off your anchor to get into a desired state. Alternatively, it can be our alter ego, which we have previously discussed.

If your physiology is like that of the cave man, I encourage you to do the internal work to take on this new posture as an immediate pick-me-up. Stand up and be seen. You are amazing. Ultimately, it will all work together for you to acknowledge yourself and see how worthy you are of the love and respect you desire. Never allow anyone else other than you to determine your worth. No one other than you is deserving or qualified to hold that position.

19 - Always Be True to You

Being true to yourself is fundamental to living an authentic life. It is this commitment to your true self that allows you to stop self-judgement. Owning your truth stems from self-love and works to develop it. It is the understanding that you are good enough just as you are. You are complete, whole, and lovable right now regardless of circumstance. Standing in your truth has its challenges. Not everyone agrees, and their judgements can hurt like hell. Just know this has nothing to do with you and everything to do with where they are in their own personal journey.

When I first ventured back into the dating scene after my divorce, I expressed feelings for a guy I was seeing at that time. It was then he decided the relationship was over. I judged myself for having shared my feelings. Maybe I shouldn't have to have kept him in my life. As time passed, I stopped judging myself and began to question why I would feel so crappy about telling someone how I felt. There is nothing wrong with telling someone you care about them, even when it scares you. On the other hand, there was also nothing wrong with his decision, either. It was simply an indication of what he was wanting at the time. The one thing I kept coming back to whenever I wanted to judge myself was that I had spoken my truth, and that was okay. You will make decisions you'll kick yourself for. Your ability to offer yourself compassion is important in these moments.

Through this rejection, I learnt a valuable lesson. Be true to yourself and what you are feeling. It is okay to be all of you. For the right person, you won't be too much or say the wrong thing. Be all of you with 100 percent authenticity. Some may hurt you because of it. Others may judge you harshly. But your soul will thank you, and your heart will grow even bigger. The learnings I have had around relationships have reminded me again and again to remain true and to not settle. Settling means I don't believe I can have what I am seeking. Being true to me has allowed me to follow my heart and honour myself.

My match is out there. Until they show up, I have dreams to chase and a life to create. I'm not sitting on the couch scrolling dating apps. Been there, done that. I am actively chasing my dreams. I trust that what is meant for me will not pass me by, and at the right time, my path will cross with that of the right person. I will simply remain true to me and my path. Trusting in the deeper knowing I have within me.

Deepening the connection to self requires you to trust and be still. To clear your mind of chatter and sit with whatever feelings and emotions come to the surface and explore them. Whether that be your intuition, or awareness, or an inner knowing you can't quite pinpoint. The more you learn about yourself and learn to love about yourself, the deeper your connection will grow. All of life will support you from this space. Your body has different needs to your soul. Get to know them both and love them equally. One is eternal, the other will take you through this mortal life. Treasure and trust them both.

Being true to yourself also comes with learning to become very good at letting go. I have noticed that so many people I met came into my life to teach me something. These lessons have generally hurt. There were times I had to continuously remind myself to not allow my heart to turn to stone, especially when it felt like my romantic relationships were simply a trail of destruction. There was one point I remember throwing my hands in the air and stating, 'I am going to die alone; fuck it all.' I had an incredible amount of love to share, and I was done with waiting for them to show up. The universe and your angels have no real concept of time, yet they know what perfect timing is. Maybe my trail of failed relationships was a sign for me to focus on my business and creative projects, including this book. I've written so much of this book while learning and stepping into greater and greater versions of me. There have been various versions of this book as I incorporated each new lesson.

One of the biggest things I have learnt from trusting the process is that it's fruitless to resist change. Resisting only means you suffer for longer. There are more tears, anger and tantrums. It is important to feel the emotions, then move on. Life will continue whether you are holding onto the pain or letting it go. I always sit with the harder emotions. Sit in the fire, so to speak. It reminds me that, as one door closes, another will always open. What comes through the next door is usually even better than what was closed behind the previous door. It is in this knowledge, and having experienced it many times, that I learnt all of life is working to my benefit. Whether I understand it or not, life is only going to become better and better if I allow it to, no matter who or what leaves. The key is to not be caught up in the drama of it, rather to allow change to enter your life and celebrate its arrival. What new and exciting things are now in store for you? Don't worry that some people will think you're crazy. That is only because they are living in the drama of what is exiting their life, rather than celebrating the greater possibilities entering their life. In all honesty, the greater your expectation, the better it is.

During challenging times, it's often hard to know what to choose and do. **Staying true to your authenticity and direction will allow you to make aligned choices.** You won't always get this right. When it does turn to shit, learn the lessons, adjust, and step into the next best version of yourself. You just become a little bit wiser. I am always using life like a mirror to look at the dark sides of myself so I can continue to adjust and grow. I look at the results that are showing up like a compass and I am continuously adjusting my course as I navigate through life. It is your ability to adapt that will set you apart. The faster you adapt, the faster you will move forward.

Learning who you are is about unlearning and letting go of everything that you are not, including the labels you have unnecessarily applied to yourself. In tearing down your belief structure about yourself and the world around you, you discover your truth. It's standing up for yourself, what you want, and being the person you want to be without having to explain why. It's getting it wrong, learning, and trying again. It's getting knocked down and standing up again and again.

I am the happiest I have ever been in my life so far, yet the heartache, pain, learning and falling continues as I move through this rapid period of growth. Through it all, I innately know that this is all happening *for* me, not *to* me. Through my pain, I can show you the faster road to success.

Life won't be simple. If you aren't learning, you aren't growing. Embrace the challenges and try not to resist change. The more you resist, the longer the pain persists. Allow yourself to feel all: the tears, the anger, the hurt. Feel all of it and get it out of your system. If you are not willing to feel and move through it, then you may store that energy in your body, only for it to be unlocked later.

When my ex-husband left, I made sure I felt everything and learnt everything I could the first time so there would be no place of pain to venture back into. People were telling me it took years to get through the emotional baggage of a marriage breakdown. I thought to myself, *fuck that*. No way am I going to give this man any more time than I must. I was not prepared to give him that level of control over my life. I was going to prove them all wrong, and I did. After about seven or eight months, people started to comment that I was saying and doing things they were only willing to step into or do after about two years. For some, it was more like four years. It was my willingness to let go of all the emotion, face every stupid thing I was telling myself—including not being lovable enough or worthy of having someone love me—that gave me my freedom. I followed my intuition, even when it continued to lead me into more pain and heartache. In the end, I cut years off the healing process by being willing to fall apart. Also know that this was only possible because I had trust in myself—in my ability to support myself and lean on others when I required it.

I learnt to be true to me and trust myself through trial and error. Seeking love and forgiveness over hate. It has been a side effect of working through the triad of self and incorporating everything in this book. It all sits on the foundation of discovering who you are at your core. It is the real you—your true soul. The being you were born to be, without all the conditioning from people and the world. Discovering your true self is about coming home to who you are and not what everyone wants or told you to be.

No matter what is happening for you, it is important to always remain true to who you are on any given day, in any given moment. Who you are is a gift, and making yourself less than, is only doing a disservice to yourself and potentially the world. You being your unique self will be the gift that so many will require. You may never have an idea of the wonderful ripple effect you will have just by shining bright. The brighter you shine, the more people you may inspire.

Shining is not always easy, especially in difficult situations where you just want to jump into complaining, bitching and sticking it back to those who have hurt you in some way. I have lost love and friendship due to people not accepting me and my newfound sparkle. Continuing to shine requires you to take the high road, because it is the right thing to do. In time, you will be prouder of yourself for choosing to be kind and speak your authentic truth. In the end, being true to yourself through the good and bad days will bring greater fulfilment because your soul will be happy.

Through the first six months of my separation, it amazes me all the small trials I faced and overcame. It's no surprise I came out much stronger. There were weeks where all these things compounded to the point where I needed to take time to recharge. My batteries were completely empty from the constant hit of stones. Tap yourself long enough in the same place and you will bruise or experience pain, and these small hits were doing just that. I remember being so grateful for all the little things that went my way, and the big things felt *huge*. The day my rental application was accepted was such an amazing step forward. I could feel even more freedom and choice coming my way, even though it scared me like hell to wonder whether I would be okay financially. Instead of worrying, I trusted in myself. I knew I could count on me to make ends meet.

During this time in my life, gratitude became paramount. No good deed went unnoticed. Well, that's what I was aiming for. The best thing about making gratitude part of your daily life is that you see with so much clarity those who give freely and with genuine kindness. You also get to see where particular actions could have been a big thing for someone, and you can congratulate them accordingly.

On hard days, celebrate getting out of bed or putting yourself first, and truly strive forward for your dreams. Often the things that need celebrating are these small moments. You never know what will come of following your dreams. All you know is that if you put time, effort, and love into it, anything can become possible. I don't want to die with regrets. This means I must face discomfort. Facing discomfort will become easier the more you do it, because your tolerance of what is uncomfortable will shift, just like fear. Demand more of yourself and you will grow to greater heights. It is a hidden benefit to being willing to chase your hopes, dreams and goals. In the long run, you become your true self.

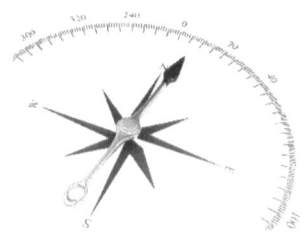

20 - The Gift of Vulnerability

Vulnerability has such a bad rap in the world today. The reason why appears to be that we fear our authentic selves. To be vulnerable requires you to connect to your heart with unwavering commitment. For a long time, I—as many do—considered vulnerability to be a weakness. I ran and hid from it. I believed that expressing my emotions—especially anger, sadness, pain and suffering—would mean that people would finally see the person I truly was. The mask I wore would be removed. I didn't want people to see that truth of who I really was. Rather, I preferred them to experience me through my mask. I now understand the incredible strength it takes to be truly vulnerable and to do it with authenticity. It takes a deep understanding of the fact that you will be okay no matter what to be authentically vulnerable. To express yourself effectively in this way requires healing and a better understanding of yourself.

The funny thing is that when someone is being truly authentic in a moment of vulnerability, some people can become uncomfortable. This is because it requires them to acknowledge and step into their own vulnerability. When it comes to someone who knows a lot about vulnerability, especially when it comes to being in a position of leadership, Brene Brown is your lady in the know. Between her TED talks on YouTube and her books, her research into the topic of vulnerability will leave you with a much greater understanding of the strength and skill required to connect with true vulnerability. It will also allow you to explore the beauty in it.

One benefit of expressing vulnerability is the level of connection that can be achieved between individuals, groups, and most importantly, the connection you have with yourself. I have found the process of getting this book onto the pages incredibly difficult at times. It required all of me to be put on display. It has taken an incredible amount of strength to connect with and express my most vulnerable moments in these chapters. I have done so in the hope that it allows you to learn from my experiences. The ability to share authentically can allow someone else to find their own heart in what you are sharing and ultimately apply it to something important to them.

You connect with vulnerability in different ways. Sometimes, it's being brave enough to express your personal stories and truth. It can be the courage to ask questions that have no middle ground. Other times, being vulnerable is about simply acknowledging how you truly feel and not hiding that from yourself or those around you. It astounds me—although it really shouldn't—how many people fail to allow themselves to express all their emotions: happy, sad, angry, and everything in between. Acknowledging your feelings is the beginning of allowing yourself to be authentic. It is simply saying, 'Here I am with all my scars. I have nothing to hide.' Being vulnerable sometimes means taking your head out of the sand and acknowledging the truth of a situation. Being honest with yourself. Ultimately, doing what is required to change the situation based on what you *can* control.

Please be aware, not everyone needs to know everything. Most of the time, it's kinder for you to have select friends who know your dark secrets, who can support you when you fall. Expressing your moments of vulnerability with the wrong person can have negative consequences, which can have you running for your Cave, setting you back considerably. Take it from me. It was a lesson I didn't learn the first time. Not even the second time. So, as they say, third time's the charm. Getting it wrong can be devastating. No matter the outcome, you will get through it. Keep being brave and stepping forward into your vulnerability and authenticity.

When you fail to find your own vulnerability, you give up the gift of a deep connection to yourself. It is possible to be vulnerable on your own, and this can be a safe place to start exploring. It all begins with the ability to sit with your heavier emotions and completely allow yourself to feel how you are feeling. It is okay for you to feel and express your full range of emotions. They are your guide. Who suddenly decided that sadness was a bad thing to express? Imagine if they took that stand on happiness too? I have been told not to be so happy because it was like I was throwing it in people's faces. Sorry, not sorry, people. Your emotions are your connection to your intuition. Your radar on what you do and don't like and even love. Love is a feeling, and we even have a day to celebrate it. You must stop judging and categorising your emotions and feelings based on what society deems acceptable. You being you in the most authentic way is also acceptable. Those who have an issue with it are yet to connect with their own vulnerability and allow their lives to expand.

There is a gift in simply allowing yourself to be in whatever state you find yourself, knowing you will be okay and can hold yourself no matter what shows up. Expressing your vulnerability allows you to grow, even if that means simply understanding yourself better.

It is too easy to push your emotions down. To put your happy mask on and just get on with the day. It is the brave person who is willing to own their shit and say, 'Hey, I am not okay.' **Vulnerability gives you the opportunity to experience all of you without judgement.** It opens your heart. In many ways, expressing yourself in this way is another form of self-love, simply because you are not judging what you are feeling. Rather, you're showing that you have learnt to accept yourself and your story in a way that allows you to trust and love yourself with ferocity. You are demonstrating to yourself that, no matter what, you have your own back, even when no one else is there to stand by your side. You stay true to you and your path.

Vulnerability goes both ways. You cannot express your own vulnerability and not be willing to receive another in their moments of vulnerability. Your inability to receive it from another person would indicate that you are yet to offer yourself a deeper level of forgiveness. Ultimate healing requires you to forgive and create a level of understanding about yourself that brings peace, no matter what life throws at you. It is the connection between logic and your emotions that allows you to bridge the gap to learning more about who you are and why you are the way you are. There are times you do not have a logical reason as to why something happened. In these moments, the clarity required to move forward comes in the form of hindsight. Other times, you simply learn something that resonates and allows greater clarity.

In my opinion, connecting with vulnerability, authenticity, and gratitude will have the biggest impact on your life. To be authentic requires you to stop worrying about judgement from others. You free yourself. It is freedom from the cage you didn't even know was around you. It is the weight suddenly lifted from your shoulders, allowing you to stand taller, be kinder, and generally more present in life. Having access to it all at the same time is the moment you take a deep breath. It nourishes your entire soul. You feel complete, and rightfully so. Through living an authentic life, you will find happiness and joy beyond what you currently believe is possible. I cannot encourage you enough to chase it, because a life worth living is one where you are happy and contributing in a way that is authentic to you. Step up and discover who you are and be willing to show that person to the world without apology. Your authentic self is a gift to the world. It is time to see and experience yourself in the same light.

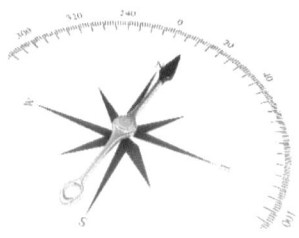

21 - Self-Care

There have been times when I have had strong points of view in relation to what self-care was and wasn't. In these moments, I was viewing self-care from a limited perspective. For everyone, self-care looks different. For some it is a massage and taking care of the body in some way. For others, it is a daily meditation practice of going in search of their higher self. For many, it is simply any activity where they can just switch off. To me, self-care can be anything that brings some level of joy and peace. I personally aim to do a combination of anything and everything depending on what my mind, body, or soul requires or leads me towards. As a standard practice, my self-care routine includes a monthly trip to the beautician and a remedial massage. I also have a regular exercise regime, which includes gentle and strenuous movement. Music forms a huge part of my daily life too, and often plays in the background at home. I also aim to take time to read a book or do an Access Bars swap—an energetic body process designed to release and ground energy.

Self-care is whatever assists in bringing balance and a sense of calm to one or many aspects of the self—mind, body, soul. In this busy world, self-care assists us to find and function from a place of alignment. To create this balance, you need to determine the right mix of activities based on what you require at the time. Balance means taking a holistic view of yourself. **You are not just a body, or a mind, or a soul; you are a combination of all these things. Each must be addressed to achieve balance.**

For the mind, seek a way to lower the volume of mental chatter, or take the time to listen to it. Listening will provide valuable insight into negative thoughts and even goals and dreams. Meditation, reading a book, working in the garden, breath techniques, and so on are all great options. It's about discovering what works for you. For some, clarity and peace of mind will come from a strenuous workout in the gym where they achieve the trio; the mind is quiet, the body is working, and they are proud of themselves. This makes them grateful for their bodies, which touches on the soul work.

I usually experience the trio if I go on a long hike. The longer the hike, the better, especially when life gets hectic or overly stressful. It gives me the time and space to work through and listen to my thoughts and let go of any points of view which aren't serving me. When I am annoyed, long hikes manage to tire me and allow me to take it out on the trail while nature nurtures me. It doesn't judge me when I cry, it simply holds that vast space for me to fall apart and put myself back together. Spending time in nature always seems to provide more than I ever could give back.

Soul work is anything that connects you with yourself or improves your triad of self. It gives you the space in which to find gratitude, love, peace, and connection to yourself and the world around you. For women, soul work provides an opportunity to step into feminine energy, which is all about receiving, letting barriers down, and opening the heart space. For men, it's stepping into their masculine energy, which is a doing, protective energy. Masculine energy doesn't have to be domineering. There is a soft, loving undertone to it.

The body component of the trio isn't anything that you don't already know: eat well and exercise. I also believe your body has its own consciousness. Many people consider this to be your gut. The health of your body is determined by your gut health. To make the most of this vessel carrying your soul around and to ensure its longevity, you must care for it. It is the same as servicing your car, cleaning your house, or maintaining anything of use. Your body is your soul's connection to this earth. When you die, your body will remain here, and your soul will continue on in whatever way you believe it does.

You cannot expect your body to care for you if you do not care for it. You don't put low quality fuel in a luxury car. Treat your body like a luxury car.

Now, this doesn't have to be all organic food, sugar-free, caffeine-free, or any of those other unbalanced "diets". Life is meant to be fun after all! We all know how we are supposed to eat: more vegetables, salads, fruit, lean meat, grains. Limiting alcohol, sugar, and refined carbs such as white bread. The best thing you can do for your health is to take a balanced approach. Start by eating foods as close to the way nature provided them. Limit the amount of processing your food goes through. This ensures it is as nutritious as possible, which makes it the premium fuel your body deserves. Chicken and salad wraps taste amazing and aim to incorporate three to four different veggies into an evening meal. Over time, you will end up craving healthier food and enjoying the taste. You will feel better as your body begins to operate more effectively. You may even find you have more energy. It's also not about changing everything, but more about how you can make your current meals more nutritious. Stop thinking skinny. Think about adding quality elements to the fuel and removing or limiting the contaminants.

I still love chocolate and savory treats like chips. Having studied nutrition, I understand the negative sides to excess sugar and its direct correlation to the cuddly bit around my middle. I also understand the dangers of saturated fat. I also know that when you tell me I can't have something, that will be all I crave. I end up binge eating it, then experiencing guilt. When I am trying to be good and come across something sweet or somewhat delicious that grabs my attention, I ask myself one thing: 'Can I have this another day?' If not, or if it's a special occasion, then I will indulge myself. If it's from a local café or the supermarket, then I can have that another day and not today. This way, I don't trigger the fear of missing out (FOMO).

When my husband left, I found myself in my own space. I noticed I didn't eat a quarter of the amount I once did. Not because I was judging myself or desiring to be thinner; I just simply didn't require it. I began to eat when hungry. The portions became smaller and smaller. In the coming months, I found I wanted to start exercising again, but not in a way designed to punish myself or to lose weight. It came from a place of doing what my body felt like doing and to assist with dealing with stress. There was no concept that I must eat breakfast, lunch and dinner, or limit certain foods. I just listened to what my body felt like eating or doing. All these things contributed to me on a soul level and therefore made me incredibly happy. The results felt like they came fast and easy, and in all honesty, how does it get better than that?

For so long, I had judged my body. I hated it. I pushed and pulled my body in every direction for it to be what the world expected it to be based on ideals created by the media. Not once before my separation had I truly connected with gratitude for how truly amazing my body was. It was only once I began to truly acknowledge and embrace all of me that my body changed, and life began to flow with greater ease. When you can act and treat your body from a place of loving all of you without any ifs or buts, you open yourself up to a greater sense of freedom and peace. This is available to everyone, yet very few choose to embrace it. Rather, most focus on fixing flaws. Ask your body what it wants to look and feel like. I can guarantee it will tell you or show you. Listen to its wisdom like you would your intuition. It will tell you everything you need to know.

Listening to your body is the greatest way you can contribute to it. I know this sounds crazy but hear me out. At first, I thought it was strange too. With time, I began to ask who else was better positioned than me to tell me what my body required. I understood what was in pain because I was the one feeling it. By intuitively listening, I could determine what it required. Please don't think I am saying doctors and other practitioners are unnecessary, because they are necessary. What I am saying, is to listen to their advice and use your own intuition to determine if it's right for you.

Acknowledging and being grateful for all of yourself and your body right now is self-care. Each aspect of self—the mind, body and soul—requires attention. In providing this for yourself, life will become richer, contain more colour, and you might experience more joy. Knowing what self-care is specifically for you is critical to meeting your personal needs. Understanding what you require will come through trial and error, so allow yourself the time and opportunities to try different things and see what works for you. You may develop a long list of things. This is wonderful because you will never get bored. Just look after your luxury vessel. Fill your mind with positive thoughts and connect with your soul, whatever that means for you. The sooner you see yourself as being beautiful, complete and luxurious as you are, the sooner you start treating yourself as such.

22 - Respect You

Respecting You is all about the way you treat yourself. From the way you move your body, to the food you eat, down to what you are saying to yourself when you don't think you're even listening. It's also present in the way you allow others to treat you. Self-respect comes down to the standards and expectations you set for yourself and the habits you're creating that are moving you in the direction of your hopes, dreams, and goals.

Whether you are aware of it or not, you will have a series of standards and expectations about each key area in your life. There are four key areas. These are: health, wealth, relationships and self. Relationships include intimate relationships, family and friendships. The self includes your hobbies and interests, as well as spiritual and emotional growth. Health is anything to do with your physical body, including your fitness. Wealth is everything to do with your financial position, what you do with money, and what your beliefs are about money, including what it means to have and to not have it.

It is important to understand what standards and expectations you have in these areas, because some may not actually be serving you. This goes for both high and low standards and expectations. Having expectations which are too high don't tend to be achievable. This means you keep falling short, which affects your self-worth. However, having expectations that are too low is also detrimental. The issue with any low standards and expectations you set is they are too easy to achieve. You don't receive the sense of achievement from getting the job done. Or you may not achieve your goals at all if you let yourself off the hook too easily.

When it comes to the standards and expectations you set for others, this has a direct link to your current level of self-respect. If you are not willing to ask for what you truly deserve, you may find yourself being taken advantage of or doing more than what is reasonable for others while forgetting to meet your own needs. When your expectations of others are too high, it damages relationships. This happens because the person doesn't feel they can achieve what you are asking of them. It isn't friends you tend to have high expectations of; it's more likely to be your family and intimate partner. There are times when you may be asking more of them than you're asking of yourself, and this simply isn't fair. As the saying goes, treat others as you expect to be treated. Along this line, have expectations of others that would be reasonable to expect of yourself.

Nothing more, nothing less. It feels terrible to be on the receiving end of high expectations, and if you're a people pleaser, it's hard to say no. Therefore, strain and pain become part and parcel of life.

On the flip side, when your expectations and standards for others are too low—another trait of a people pleaser—you will never ask for what you truly require. You may find it difficult to ask for help, full stop. You will work yourself ragged for very little reward. It's a vicious cycle that leaves you exhausted and questioning your worth. When you have low expectations of others, the likelihood of having a low triad of self increases as you go above and beyond to have people like and approve of you.

If I were to stereotype, I would say that those who have high expectations of others operate from their ego, hiding their personal pain behind their ego. They hold low expectations of themselves to continue to feel safe, while expecting more from others. Having a low expectation of self means they will always meet their own expectations, allowing them to remain in the ego state. Having high expectations of others means others will fall short, which also provides the ego with a boost. They also require others to fill the gap so they can get what they want. They can be described as "high maintenance" or "needy".

Individuals who are highly driven can have excessively high standards for themselves. This continues to move them forward, striving for higher and higher levels of success in whatever they are focused on. This is both positive and negative. If the timelines don't support a balanced approach, burn out and adrenal fatigue become real possibilities, especially when self-inflicted stress is experienced over a long period of time. I have personally fallen into this category. Whilst I had high expectations of myself, I still had low expectations of those around me. It was a whole learning journey to discover I could let myself off the hook and still achieve my goals, along with raising my expectations of those around me. It is one thing to demand things of yourself. **Putting yourself in the position to openly discuss your needs of another requires you to connect with vulnerability and be honest, even in the face of possible rejection.** As challenging as it can be, it is a necessary step when looking to improve your self-respect. It's the process of putting the lesson into action to change the situation.

It probably sounds quite complicated to break it all down into possible personality types, but it's quite simple. What are you willing to accept and what won't you accept from both yourself and others? It can be as simple as asking a partner to cook more to share the workload. Sometimes when we start to ask for more, there can be pushback from the other party. Maybe it's because they're not willing to pick up the slack. Or they may feel that your expectations of them are now too high. This is where you need to be open to discussing it rather than just expecting them to come to the party. It may be that there are other tasks that can be shared, so both parties feel as though they have had a win. This is the best outcome you can look for, unless, of course, you have someone with high expectations of you and low expectations of themselves. This is when you might need to put on your boxing gloves and stand up for yourself.

Respecting yourself within a new intimate relationship can also provide challenges. You will have the pull of your more primal sexual desires along with your heart. When I first started meeting new people, I noticed I was too willing to accept less and disrespected myself in the process to hold their attention. So, I began to look at how I was getting there. The outcome wasn't anything unexpected, but I needed to consciously look at it and ask more of myself and the relationships I was seeking. I learnt I really wasn't cut out for a casual relationship. My heart was too big, and it wanted to find a safe place to call home. I needed to set a new standard and stay away from "situationships", otherwise I was asking for more of the same—heartache. I would continue to question why I wasn't good enough for them to want to keep, even though I knew I had a lot to offer.

Ultimately, it was about me acknowledging my worth and showing myself the respect I wanted to receive. Which meant a lot of rejection. When it came to relationships, it then became about them demonstrating to me through their actions that they saw my worth.

Your standards and expectations are in everything you do, so don't expect that looking at them will be sorted in an afternoon. It is a progressive process that requires application. To begin identifying the gap in the four key areas of health, wealth, relationships, and self, start by taking some time to consider each area and think about what you would love that area of your life to look like. In this way, it's like goal setting. It is through identifying the gap that you will start to recognise where your standards might be too low or too high. You can adjust accordingly and create a better result. Some of these will be easy, some will be hard.

Once you have reviewed the standards and expectations you hold in the four key areas, you can generate better habits to create an even more amazing life. For an easy example, if you want to improve your health and don't currently exercise, you may look to improve by including thirty minutes of exercise three times a week. Aim to consistently meet this standard. Your habits determine the quality of your life. From the moment you open your eyes each morning, you can find yourself on autopilot. What is the very first thing you consciously feel or say when you wake up? Are you looking forward to the day ahead or dreading it? These initial feelings and thoughts will set up the rest of your day. There are days when shit has been hitting the fan in the days prior, and I won't be waking up as vibrantly as I usually would. I can almost guarantee that unless I do something about it—and quickly—it will determine how the rest of my day goes. Start the day with low energy, and you will likely feel this way most of the day. Jump out of bed excited for what the day will bring, and you will have a high-energy day. This is where connecting with gratitude can be very powerful. It is heart-centred and invites you to notice even more things to be grateful for.

Waking up in a crappy mood happens to all of us. What is important is how you change it up to improve your day. I love upbeat music, so I have found some fun playlists on YouTube and Spotify that make me want to get up and dance in the kitchen.

The more awareness you can bring into your daily life and the more you can tap into a deeper understanding of what makes you tick, the more you are able to act in alignment and with respect for yourself. Mind, body and soul require respect. Bring these components of yourself together and I promise you, you will feel joy on a more consistent basis. When in doubt, trust. You have guides to help you on your way. All you need to do is listen—just maybe not with your ears.

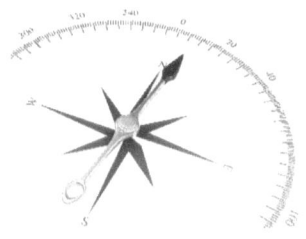

23 - You are Never Alone

There are times during the self-development journey that you feel like a lone little fish in a vast pond. You find yourself in limbo. You know too much to go back and are not yet firmly placed into your future. I found myself in this place of limbo many times for varying periods of time. One of the reasons was that I had raised the expectations of those I wanted in my life. I was seeking my soul tribe. When I started this journey, I noticed how many people were still on the victim train, hiding in their Caves. The world suddenly felt big, and I felt alone. I was looking to be surrounded by fun, light-hearted people, and I needed to discover where they hung out. What I learnt was you don't need to search for these people. You find one another. Sometimes in unusual circumstances. Who you are in your day-to-day life will attract your tribe. **You are an incredible magnet attracting people and situations that are a match to who you are.** From a growth viewpoint, this is where you can use life as a mirror to measure outcomes. You can compare what you want in your life to what is showing up. Become what you are wanting to attract. So, what are you attracting into your life and is it what you want? If not, what do you need to change to have the life you're seeking?

This journey can be tough, and even the most seasoned individuals have their moments where they too struggle and wonder if it's all worth it. It's the ability to get knocked down again and again and continue to stand up stronger, wiser, and more committed to your dreams than ever, that makes the individual. These falls can feel exceptionally lonely, and often you are unsure who to turn to. The old friends on the victim train are still stuck in their Cave and just don't see the world the same as you do. This makes it difficult to obtain the advice you may require, and if you do ask, the advice you receive usually isn't that helpful.

In these times of loneliness, it's comforting to know that you are never alone. The more I have learnt about the physical and non-physical—what you can and can't see—the less alone I feel in my dark moments. I believe every person has their own team of angels waiting to be asked for help. You would be doing them an injustice by not asking. It would be as if you were ignoring their very existence and desire to assist you in your life's journey. If you don't ask, you don't receive. Ever heard that before? Maybe they hid it in the Bible so you wouldn't believe it. There are other angels too. Archangels and all other types of light beings that can heal us, hold us in our times of need, and support us in creating our wildest dreams. Whether you ask or not, they are still working to keep you on track. They might slow you down or smack you over the head to help you learn something. This is their role: to ensure you stay on purpose, so you learn what you came into this life to discover. You are never off track; you are always precisely where you are meant to be. If you were supposed to be anywhere else, you would be there.

So, how do you know when an angel is guiding you? Well, repetitive numbers are just one sign—more on this in the following chapter. Feathers are another. A chance encounter with someone. There is a huge amount of faith and trust that goes into following the signs. This trust is built not only in them but also in yourself and knowing you're not crazy. The trust is built over time and experience. Sometimes, something just doesn't feel right, and you have no idea why. Other times, the thing that does feel right is uncomfortable or scary as hell. It's in these moments you need to trust and simply do it anyway, even when it makes no sense. Sometimes, this is about meeting commitments you have previously made that are important for you to see through. To get a general sense of it all, imagine you are blindfolded, and all you have to follow is your gut feeling. You may run into a few poles, but you will always end up where you are meant to be. Is it time to put more faith in yourself and less in the people around you to tell you what you should or shouldn't do? What does your gut say?

There was a point in my life when I was asking constantly, 'What am I here to do?' I had a sense that there was more for me to be and achieve, but I just couldn't put my finger on it. I was asking desperately, for what felt like ages. Ironically, I was not seeing the signs. It took my Facebook news feed filling up with ads for the Coaching Institute for me to finally pick up on the 'hint' that I was to investigate it. I can now see how perfectly coaching has shaped and filled my life, allowing me to grow astronomically. I also see that it was not the end point, it was simply the next stepping stone. This will also be true for you in your journey. The next thing will always be leading you across the stream. Sometimes your feet will get wet. Other times, it will be easier.

Following your passion or path is not always easy. At times, it requires taking a blind leap of faith, trusting it will turn out exactly the way it's meant to. Let me use this book as an example: Since I was very young, I had always known I would write a book. Every time I had previously sat down and started to write, I found it was never the book I truly wanted to write—that was, until this book. I can't tell you why, but I know that now is the time to be putting these words on these pages.

Writing this book has challenged me, my marriage, my friendships, and my priorities in many ways. To write this book has required blind faith in me. Trusting what I know in my heart to be true and valuable to share. Trusting also in my life's journey and my angels and guides.

I have a favourite poem called 'Footsteps in the Sand' that outlines how God and our angels walk with us. I discovered this poem when I was about eighteen, and I have loved it ever since. It is about a man walking along the beach next to God. The man looks back over his lifetime and he notices that at the hardest times in life there was only one set of footprints. He questions God as to why, in his hours of need, he was alone. God responded that it was in those moments the man was being *carried* by God. This always tugs my heartstrings and reinforces my belief that you are never truly alone. All we must do is ask and be open to what shows up. The trick with this is to not assume *how* it will show up. Be open to the magic, because it never looks the way we imagine. As a belief, this thinking is shaping my world in a magical way, and I'm okay with that.

There is a story about a man who has fallen into the sea from a ship, and he keeps asking for God to save him. Boats and other forms of rescue arrive, but he turns each away, stating that God will save him. The man ultimately drowns, and when he is in front of God, he asks why God didn't come and rescue him. God says, 'I sent boats and other forms of rescue, but you didn't take what I offered.' Now if that isn't the biggest slap over the head from the hand of God, I don't know what is. The moral of this story is that we can become so hung up on how something *should* be or what it *should* look like that we miss the actual opportunity presenting itself. There is more than one way to skin a cat.

Follow your gut even when it feels like it's taking you on a side road or wild goose chase, because it will always lead you back to the main path. Remove from your mind that your path is a straight line. It's not, and there will be times when you feel like you do a full three-sixty. Even with the twists, turns, and sometimes redirections, you will still always be on track.

It can be hard not to become hung up on how something will happen. Humans are designed to want to control situations to feel more comfortable. You worry about all the things you don't need to worry about. Experience shows it probably won't even happen. Imagine if you spent less time worrying about the worst-case scenario and simply trusted that whatever was meant for you would show up in the most perfect way. I too am guilty of this. It isn't always easy to trust and give control to something you can't even see. This is the pain, the journey, and the gift of true surrender. Give your fears to God. It's about letting go of control, trusting, and having faith. The most ironic part of it all is that when you allow yourself to do this, your life is so much better. Instead of spending time in fear, stress, and worry, you can put your faith in a greater source and simply go with the flow. Hold your intention and take any relevant action. Generally, this means you can be so much happier and a whole lot less stressed. Sitting where I do now on my own journey, I can say with a great deal of certainty that life is about joy, learning, and growing.

I always come back to this concept of, 'What if the purpose of life was to be ridiculously happy?' To be ridiculously happy requires you to heal from the pain and suffering in your heart and mind. To give up the idea of being a victim. To create the direction of your life, while leaving space for divine guidance. To remove the need for control and instead, trust both yourself and something greater. To live life from the place where everything is in abundance. To allow life's lessons and learn what it is you came here to learn. Ultimately, to discover the core of who you are and live in that truth with love, joy, and gratitude. Imagine how amazing and simple life would be then.

24 - Signs From Above

Through my journey, I have taken many different viewpoints on the subject of God. To be honest, I'm still not 100 percent sure if he, she, they, or it, really does exist. What I do believe is there is something out there with whom we sat down and decided what we wanted to learn in this life. We outlined the lessons we wanted to learn, and from there the wheels were put in motion as to planning out the best ways to learn those lessons. If I look at my past and all the challenges I have faced, this point of view helps me make sense of things. Otherwise, why the hell did I have to go through it all?

As humans, we have this desire to know what and why things happen. We need to give it meaning. It's one of the things that changed within our brains during the evolutionary process. Your brain developed the capacity to understand and determine meaning from events and circumstances and to categorise them. As wonderful as this is, there are times when not having to give meaning or search for patterns would make life easier to handle.

Angels and spirits are everywhere around you, guiding and listening to you. Some people fear them, but for me, they bring comfort. I guess, having lost so many people early in my life, it's nice to know you're never truly alone and that loved ones live on in one way or another. There is no reasonable explanation for when I feel something sit on the end of my bed, stroke my hair, or shake me awake at night, but I also know that I feel intense love at these times. It's also comforting to know there is someone who knew me guiding me through life.

Some people collect feathers during their day, seeing them as symbolic in some way. I love the white fuzzy ones. I logically know they come from birds, but symbolically to me, these feathers are left by angels. Reminding me they are walking with me at every moment. One day, I was walking out of a shop and as if by magic, one caught my eye as it fluttered on down in the light breeze. There was another instance where I was stepping into some courage and recording a message from a deceased individual, when a large white feather floated down in front of me where I sat at the school car park. Your guides are with you always, and they are waiting for you to allow them to contribute to your life. You must simply be open to allowing them to work their magic. You don't have to be psychic to connect with angels. Everyone can do it. It's about looking for and understanding the signs.

I have lots of angelic symbols in my life, including Kookaburras, Willy Wagtails, as well as the previously mentioned feathers and repetitive numbers. For those who may not know, seeing specific numbers, such as '111' repeated in different areas and times of your life, indicates the beginning of a spiritual journey or awakening. All numbers, and sometimes combinations such as '888', '777' or even '711', have significant meanings. These are all signs and messages from your angels. Each number has a different meaning. There are so many people who are sceptical about this. The world is full of endless possibilities. What are the chances of seeing multiple cars, potentially in a row, with '888' on them? This has happened to me on various occasions. I think the most car number plates with the same three digits I have seen in a row are three cars with '333'. If you find you're seeing the same numbers all the time, Google it. You may be surprised at what you read or how relevant it might be to your life.

I have included the table following as a quick reference guide. I've put in bold what I've found each number to mean based on how I've understood them in my life.

For you, the meanings may differ, so be sure to connect with your own intuition to determine what is true for you.

No.	Meaning
1	**Life purpose**

New beginnings, creation, independence, uniqueness, love, inspiration, attainment, glory, happiness, fame, fulfilment, omniscience, and creating your reality.

2	**Balance**

Service and duty, balance and harmony, adaptability and diplomacy, co-operation and consideration, receptivity and love. Number 2 also relates to partnerships and relationships, intuition and insight, faith and trust, and your divine life purpose and soul mission.

3	**Mind, body and soul connection**

Communication and self-expression, adventure, inspiration and creativity, humour, optimism and joy, spontaneity, and enthusiasm. Number 3 also symbolises the principle of growth, expansion and abundance on the mental, emotional, financial and spiritual levels.

Number 3 is the number of manifesting and manifestation and carries the vibration of the Ascended Masters.

4	**You are protected; goals and passions; the four sacred elements**

Protection of the angels, mastery, building solid foundations, determination, production and hard work, inner wisdom, security, self-control. Number 4 also represents our passion and drive and encourages us to work harmoniously yet diligently to achieve our goals and aspirations.

Number 4 is the number that represents the four elements of Air, Fire, Water and Earth, and the four sacred directions, North, South, East and West. Number 4 also resonates with the energies of the archangels.

No.	Meaning
5	**Change**
	Personal freedom, non-attachment, change, life lessons learned through experience, release and surrender, influence, sensuality, promotion and making positive life choice and decisions.
6	**Keep your thoughts positive**
	Unconditional love, balance and harmony, home and family, honesty and integrity, adjustment, problem solving, seeing clearly, teaching, convention, curiosity, peace and peacefulness, grace and dignity, simplicity. Number 6 signifies the need for stability in all aspects of your life.
7	**Your angels are with you and congratulating you**
	'Collective Consciousness', faith and spirituality, spiritual awakening and awareness, spiritual enlightenment, spiritual acceptance and development, intuition and inner-knowing, psychic abilities, deep contemplation, natural healer and healing, ritual, peace, alchemy.
8	**Abundance**
	Authority and personal power, self-confidence, executive ability, confidence, inner-strength, professionalism and the professional, material freedom, success, good judgement, money, finances, riches, manifesting wealth, abundance and prosperity, provision, giving and receiving, thoroughness, self-reliance, stability, good judgement and problem solving.
9	**Endings and conclusions; bringing about new beginnings**
	Universal love, eternity, faith, Universal Spiritual Laws, Karma, spiritual enlightenment, spiritual awakening, service to humanity, humanitarianism and the humanitarian, light working and lightworkers, leading by positive example,

No.	Meaning
	philanthropy and self-sacrifice, selflessness, destiny, soul, purpose and mission, a higher perspective, self-love, freedom, popularity, optimism and divine wisdom.

I have encouraged my girls to notice the signs, and they understand these are from the angels who guide us. We used to play a game on car trips, noticing what repeating numbers we could see on number plates, and then later we would look up their meanings. It was also interesting to notice that the numbers we each saw were different. As much as this isn't scientific proof, I don't feel I need proof. Sometimes the possibility of magic makes life so much more beautiful, intriguing, and special.

Never doubt your intuition. You are experiencing that awareness for a reason. The number of times I've kicked myself because I didn't follow my intuition, and if I had, I would have been saved from some form of grief... This can be as simple as a feeling to take a certain road as you're driving along. Usually, there's less traffic that way, or maybe it's a smoother ride. With intuition, you don't understand why until after the fact. Then it's like, 'Oh, okay. Now I get why I was supposed to do that.' Sometimes, it's so you can meet someone in particular or so you can discover something that becomes useful later. Everything leads to another thing. Follow those nudges and energetic strands. It can be like a fun game of 'Where will this odd idea take me?' Life becomes more of an adventure.

25 - Stay in the Question

How many times have you decided something needed to be a particular way, and then when all was said and done, it wasn't the best option? Being in the question means continually seeking different answers, without getting stuck in how something is supposed to be. **A great question is, 'What else is possible?' This invites greater and greater possibilities. And your brain is always on the lookout for opportunities.**

It is incredibly tempting to seek certainty, to try to understand or come to conclusions about things, even when following those intuitive nudges. Sometimes, rather than waiting to see where something will take you, you want to know where you're going first. Unfortunately, this is not always how it works. As a result, you move away from asking questions that open possibilities in life. When you ask questions such as, 'What else is possible?' or 'What will this create?' you open yourself to receiving magic, and you don't limit outcomes. When you decide what something is going to be, you stop following the energetic strands of possibility. Conclusion is made up of judgement. When you remove judgement, all you are left with is options.

I challenge you to judge nothing for one week and rather consider any judgement as an interesting point of view. Become the observer. When you're the observer, you can be more objective in your point of view. Observe not only others but yourself as well. Asking questions such as, 'Why did I react like that?' allows you to *observe* rather than *react.* Stepping back takes you out of the emotion. Emotion creates so much of the drama and pain. So often, judgement makes situations worse. It can have you concluding that things didn't happen for your greater good just because they didn't turn out as you decided they should.

Being an observer generally means you don't need to say as much. The ego hates this simply because it seeks significance, which it does not receive from taking a back seat. Your ego wants to be right.

Staying in the question also allows you to notice greater possibilities both about yourself and any situation you're in. When you are bogged down in a conclusion, you have limited the possibilities to your current level of thinking. Albert Einstein said the thinking that created a problem cannot also solve it. Observing takes you away from thinking and offers you the opportunity to step into the state of allowing things. In allowing things, there is no judgement. There is simply the perspective that what happened was interesting.

I tend to ask or direct many of my questions to my angel guides. I feel my way to possible answers based on what feels light or heavy. Truth will always feel lighter, while a lie will feel heavy. You can try this too.

Exercise

Ask your body to give you a read on whether it likes tomatoes, for example. Your brain already knows the answer to this one, so you shouldn't have to contend with the brain putting up any barriers. Make sure you are connecting with your body. It may help to take several slow deep breaths first. Put a hand on the area around your sternum and the other on your stomach while you breathe, this will assist with creating a connection to your body. Ask a variety of questions, some which you know the answer to, until you notice the light or heavy feelings in your body. Once you are feeling comfortable with this, begin asking other questions you may not know the answer to and see what shows up. Again, do not have a point of view in relation to the answer, let it simply be interesting. The more you utilise this practise, the clearer you will become with your answers.

When you have Tarot Cards read, or any form of spiritual

reading, you are asked to come with a question based on what you are wanting to know. So, asking questions shouldn't be such a strange concept. It doesn't matter whether you choose to access this information or trust someone else. Keep your questions open. For example, rather than asking if a specific person is who you are meant to spend your life with, ask to know more about the individual who is to fulfill this role. This way, you have the rest of the world's population from which to choose, rather than receiving a 'yes' or 'no'. This is a prime example of the possibility that comes from being in the question rather than conclusion. The possibilities available to us in this lifetime are extensive. The possibilities our minds can perceive are exceptionally limited and can only be based on experience. Imagine if the most amazing things that were meant for you, your brain couldn't perceive simply because it didn't know how much greater things could be?

I experienced this when my ex-husband left. I thought he was the duck's nuts only to realise very quickly that there were more incredible men out there. I just didn't know they were even a possibility because I thought I had experienced the best. Then began the slippery learning slope. When the first guy ended it, I was sad. How could it possibly get better than that? He was everything I could have hoped for. He watched a movie with me and rubbed my leg. Pretty low standard, hey? Well, guess what? The next guy was better, and so was the next one. They just kept getting better and in different ways. This process forced me to acknowledge just how *abundant* the universe was and how *limited* my expectations were due to my past experiences. Now I apply this trust not just to my relationships but to every area of my life. I now have an expectation that things are going to become even more amazing every single day, even if by the smallest of margins. Not every day is perfect. There are still many days that bring me down. Then I pick up the learnings and power on. My goal these days is to learn things the first time. Repeating lessons is the head slap I try to avoid. I focus on the onwards and upwards, and I keep my radar on for new possibilities, even when they scare the shit out of me.

Being open to what else could create wonderful things in your life allows you to go with the flow and release the reigns of control. **Questions minimise resistance, meaning wonderful things can enter your life.** It also lessens the emotional response when things exit your life. If not this, then what? Play with asking questions and receiving responses, testing out what makes you feel lighter and heavier. Always follow what makes you feel lighter, even when it's uncomfortable to do so.

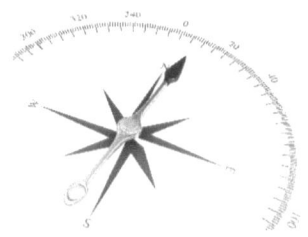

26 - Is Self-Judgement Stealing Your Peace?

Self-judgement can hold you back from having everything you want. It can be the hidden anchor that drags you backward. It has a sneaky habit of showing up and stealing your joy without you even noticing.

When my ex called it off, I was a mess. I cried, judged and blamed myself for months. I drank copious amounts of wine and hid in my room. I cried the hardest during the moments of self-blame. I was taking hardcore ownership of the marriage breaking down, meaning I took 100 percent ownership, as if it were solely my fault. But I was failing to acknowledge myself and what I had achieved. For the last few years of my marriage, I was openly grateful to my ex for being there for me. In hindsight, I see that he did not have the same level of gratitude for me. The paradigm it created was that I made him greater than me, more important than me and my goals and dreams. I put everything on the backburner as I tried to work out if I was going to put it all into my breaking marriage—which may have involved giving up on my dreams—or ride the wave to allow change to ripple through my life.

It wasn't until a friend pointed out to me that it was he who was unhappy with me that I was able to put everything into perspective and stop taking all the blame. Once I was able to release the blame, there was no turning back. Only one heck of an adventure ahead of me. It scared me to death and excited me to my core. What was now truly possible for me in my life? This was the space I could sense when he initially ended the marriage. It's important to note there is a difference between taking ownership and blaming yourself. **Blame lends itself to judgement and self-hate. Taking ownership, however, is about finding solutions and moving forward.** When I was taking ownership, I had not disconnected from the guilt and blame. I was in the perpetual cycle of self-judgement without the forward movement.

When you're judging and blaming yourself, you can easily give up on what's important to you. It's this which stops you from living your best life. Prioritising the need to fit in and making others more comfortable by playing a small game is not honouring you. I began the process of giving up worrying about what people thought of me as I grew and began chasing my dreams. At times, I do still struggle with it. When you have big dreams, it requires you to give up parts of yourself. Grow through the experience, give up more, grow again.

The process continues. Now, this is also true with wanting to live your most joyful life. People would ask me what I was on to be so happy all the time. Imagine if instead of owning my joy, I stepped away from being my authentic and openly happy self to make others more comfortable. It seems crazy, but we do it all the time. When it comes to happiness, people don't seem able to recognise what's right in front of them anymore. It has become strange and weird to see someone who is genuinely happy, and this indicates a sad truth within society. When did we forget to be happy, despite the challenges?

At the time my marriage ended, I didn't realise just how unhappy I was. We were the dream couple to many of our friends, but as it turned out, neither of us were happy. Soon after the separation, what would have been our eleven-year wedding anniversary rolled around. I recall messaging my ex and thanking him for being brave enough to end it, because I now had more of me. He messaged me back to see if I was being sarcastic or whether I meant it. The person who wrote that message and the person I was the day he left were already worlds apart. I fell hard and I grew fast. I was completely allowing myself to fall apart so I could release, heal, and find my joy again. This seems to be how I do most things in life. Let's get through this shit as fast as possible so I can get back to living and experiencing the joy life has to offer.

When in the habit of people pleasing, you tend to judge yourself the harshest. This is because you're concerned about how your behaviour and actions will affect the way others perceive you. So often, the joy and happiness from life is given away to the requirement to meet the needs or expectations of others. Imagine not living a life based on what you believe other people think you should be, do, have, or want. Instead, first follow what you want to do, be, or have. What if the only person you ever had to keep happy was yourself and it didn't matter if you were a mum, a wife, a daughter, or a sister. These roles are just labels used to categorise. They do not define you. What if you were simply you and didn't judge yourself for it? What if you didn't judge others for their choices, either? How much more freedom would you have to simply be yourself, openly and freely.

People who know me personally are aware that nothing is too far from the gutter. Sexual innuendo is hilarious. I don't take life too seriously, and outrageous laughter comes naturally. I like to have fun, and I don't give a damn what other people think as long as I am respectful and stay true to my authentic self. If I want to pretend to be a whale or dolphin splashing around at the beach, arms tucked into my sides as my bottom half flops around, then that is what I am going to do. And I'll have a cracker of a time doing it.

I recently went to the beach with my youngest daughter, and

there was a section of sand that had been washed away, leaving a slope. So, we grabbed the boogie board and started pushing each other down the slope, trying to make it all the way to the water. We had a great time. You could see so many adults wanting to connect to this type of inner child activity, yet no one did. How many times have you regretted not doing something due to a fear of what people would think? This kills more fun and dreams than actual obstacles ever could. Life is meant to be about fun and creating memories. **Live large and outrageously. Bring more fun and joy into your life.**

Choosing to be outrageously yourself does open you up to possible judgement from others. Overcoming this is part of learning to love all of you, even the fun, quirky traits. When you fail to live authentically, you may end up regretting it. Joy comes when we can openly express ourselves and feel safe to do so.

Regret usually occurs when you allow judgement—either from yourself or others—to dictate your actions. If I gave up on every book idea, online program, or business venture, I wouldn't be anywhere near the person I am today. The challenges each one of these situations created allowed me to grow and learn, each time moving further and further away from the concerns of what others thought of me. It moved me closer to my authentic self. I even teach my kids this lesson: that it doesn't matter what others think of you.

What will have the greatest impact is what you think of yourself.

Believe in you more than you need another to believe in you. Then you're well on your way to personal freedom. Just make sure it's not egotistical freedom. Instead, connect with the heart and enjoy genuine freedom. The ego is a false sense of self. Use it when required but grow beyond the requirement to use it.

The braver you are willing to be, the more willing you'll be to step into the most authentic version of yourself. This will always lead you to living a full life. I don't plan on lying in my deathbed wishing I had done something more or tried to create more. I will tell people how I feel, even if it means there is a chance my heart will be hurt. Running from fear and pain will only lead you to regret, so be brave. To be brave also means to heal and give yourself permission to live an authentic life full of love and connection. This alone is an incredible thing to aim for every single day.

Each moment of every day is a precious gift. Spend time with sick children and they will show you the true meaning of life. They are often the happiest, bravest, most resilient super souls you will ever meet. They have a different perspective on life, and we can learn a great deal from them. If you didn't know how long you had left to live, what would you choose to do differently? Knowing that, with the law of averages, you still have many wonderful years ahead of you, why are you not ticking things off the bucket list? Do those things that would make a short life worth living. Time on Earth isn't guaranteed; why wait for a health scare to decide to truly start living? Each moment is a choice, every experience an opportunity. Start viewing your world from a more expansive point of view rather than through the lens of judgment. Judgement will not give you the freedom you truly desire.

27 - Failure to Launch

Growing up, I watched a movie called *Failure to Launch*. It was about a guy who was still living at home, and his mother did everything for him. The long and short of it is he fell for a girl who made him grow up and get into creating his own life. I refer to failing to launch from the aspect of healing to find happiness. **People fail to launch if they resist healing on a deeper level.** Discovering the areas in their life in which they're holding themselves back from experiencing authentic happiness, joy, and reaching their full potential.

It is widely accepted that happiness should be created by people, situations, and things. Marketing tells you that unless you have the latest gadget, gizmo, car, clothes, weight-loss program and so on, you will be unhappy. All these things are outside of you. True happiness comes from within. It emanates from within your soul and can be accessed at any moment. Think about the last time you felt happy seemingly for no reason. Funnily enough, there is a tendency to be very self-conscious about this. You almost feel bad about it. As I've said, I have even had someone tell me to rein my happiness in because I was throwing it in people's faces.

Authentic joy is not a bad thing. Even if people around you are having a bad day, it can be nice to see a kind, smiling face to remind you not all of life is bad. When you were a child, did you ever feel amazing just because the sun was shining? In these moments, you were truly living as you chased the simple adventures of life, your soul sung loud, and you never wanted to go home. As much as these situations are outside of you, it comes down to a choice to embrace every moment. That's what makes those memories so joyful and special.

As an adult, finding happiness can seem a little harder. There are the chores and to-do lists, and the demands don't seem to end. Adults live their lives in the shadow of their joyous childish adventures, only experiencing them when reminiscing about the carefree fun of the past. Children are encouraged to hold onto their youth, to not grow up fast, to keep their sense of fun and innocence. But as adults, we don't embrace our childlike nature. That carefree freedom you so desperately seek was always and will forever be available to you. You simply need to go within and choose to embrace it. Relax a little and know that the to-do list will never end, so take time to have fun along the way.

I once went to a brewery to have lunch with friends. It was a family-friendly place with a huge grassy hill that led down to a playground and grassed area. My kids were starting to hang off me, so I suggested they go and roll down the hill because the playground was closed due to COVID-19 restrictions. I could tell they were a little apprehensive from the way they were looking around, and I could also tell they were anxious about standing out from the crowd. Already stepping into that adult way of life at the ages of nine and ten. So, I said, 'Well, let's go, then.' So off I went with my kids to roll down the hill. I had completely forgotten how sick and dizzy you get from rolling downhill, especially after cider. I laughed and laughed all the way down, ran back up once the dizziness had subsided, and rolled down again. I noticed that other kids were beginning to join us. Adults were looking on, encouraging their young ones to join.

When you are being the outward expression of fun and joy, it's wonderful to see how it rubs off on others. You see the gift you can truly be in everyday moments. Some will judge you harshly, others will want to join you. Others won't be able to move past their own fear of judgement to join you. And others will be too wrapped up in their own lives to even notice what you are doing. Life is simply a series of events and choices. **You get to choose how you experience life, whether to be serious, sad, silly, or embrace any other emotional state.** They are all just options.

Gratitude changed my life in so many incredible ways. It was not just about being grateful for the money in my bank account, the people I met, and the opportunities that allowed me to create an incredible life. It was through gratitude that I learnt to love who I was, which allowed me to be me without apology. Hence, I was able to roll down a hill carefree of others opinions of me. Gratitude set me free from the misconception that I was a victim and had no control in my life. As much as gratitude doesn't give you control of others or situations, what it does give you is a way of behaving that doesn't come from external triggers or the ego. Rather, it comes from your heart. Gratitude, when explored on a deep soul level, will transform every area of your life.

Through gratitude, I was able to find the courage and willingness to forgive people who had done wrong by me and my family. Including the man who tried to take my grandfather's money, and the lady who sold many of my father's possessions after he passed. I have applied it to my mum, understanding that everyone is doing the best they can with the tools they have at their disposal. Some of us have more tools than others, and I am always open to learning and applying new tools that enrich my life. The benefit of undergoing the process of forgiveness with anyone you are still holding residual anger or hurt towards is that you give yourself permission to let go. It is through letting go that you release the story, energetic ties to the person—which are generally negative—and all the other external triggers. This means when a situation arises that is similar in any way, you don't have to react the way you did before. Heal enough and you won't react at all. You become the observer rather than stay at the mercy of the situation or others' behaviour.

By forgiving, you are not forgetting. To forget who has hurt you and what they did would be like putting your head in the sand. You are not an ostrich, so don't be one. There seems to be this line of thinking around forgiveness that doesn't serve us. It's that to forgive someone for something, you also need to forget what they did. "Forgive and forget" has become severely misconstrued. To simply forget means that you may have missed the gold in the lesson learnt. Awareness is gold, being naive is not. I believe the true meaning behind the forgetting part is more about putting it out of your mind, so it doesn't dominate your thoughts. If you're still ruminating—having continued negative thoughts about something that don't seem to go away—then there is more to learn, or deeper forgiveness required. Give yourself time as you work through the emotions around forgiveness. Leave no stone unturned.

During my separation, it took time to work through the emotions and eventually forgive. I noticed in reflection that he did things that hurt me. The reason I was allowing this to continue was to keep him in my life. The irony was that I didn't want him back. It was a subconscious action after being together for sixteen years. So when I was able to truly disconnect, I was able to start moving forward in life. I started to write this book again. I had more space in my world for me and the things that I wanted to create. As a result, I was so much happier and the drama that occasionally followed didn't bother me as much. It was water off a duck's back. It simply slipped away.

There is much to be said for gratitude. It allows you to connect with authentic happiness which isn't subject to anyone or anything. It is pure, kind, and full of the deepest love. You will know when you have truly connected with gratitude. It will cause your heart to swell and tears to well in your eyes. What is also beautiful is that you can create and connect to this level of gratitude for yourself as you grow and heal. Be grateful for yourself and who you are in the world. I am grateful for the way I choose to show up in the world. To be the walking example of a new possibility. The light willing to touch the lives of others in a genuine, transformative way. To provide the space for you to connect with your authentic self. **This desire comes from deep within my soul and emanates from my heart with every beat.**

When you choose to grow and strive towards your potential, it is impossible not to launch. Remember to reach for the moon, even if you fail you fall amongst the stars.

Choose today to heal deeply and profoundly. It all starts with the willingness to go deep within and sit with the uncomfortable parts of yourself. Be willing to fall apart and put yourself back together in a whole new way, without the judgement. Fear will always be present. Let go of all the "shoulds" and "coulds". They are wasted energy. There are new things to be and to create. Get out of the past and into your future. More importantly, live in the present moment. That is where life is happening, right this very moment.

You cannot hate the situations that shaped you. Be grateful for them. These have been your opportunities to grow and flourish.

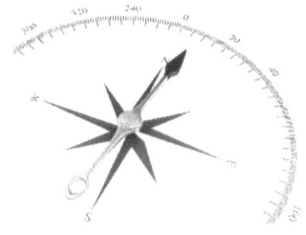

28 - Tomorrow is Uncertain

Life is a funny thing. Just when you think you know what's going to happen, it changes. There are two certainties in life: that life is uncertain, and that fear will always be present. One minute you are cruising along. The next minute, something happens that has the potential to completely shift and change the course of your life. You never know when your last day on earth will be. You are on a countdown to death, and you have no idea when it will arrive.

I wish I had something deep and meaningful to add at this point, but in all honesty, I really don't. The quality of your life is based on the decisions you make moment-by-moment, day-by-day. Every day may seem the same, yet when we look back, everything is completely different. Day-by-day, you go about your business making what you may deem to be small choices. But these small choices are compounded by the addition of minutes, hours, days, weeks, months and years. Small daily decisions can have a huge impact on your life in the long term. Every small step forward is moving you closer to success and will be what assists you in creating an incredible life.

Often, the unpopular choices have the biggest impact. They make you nervous and force you out of your comfort zone. Following that gut feeling, the synchronicities, or anything else you sense guiding you. The opinions of others do nothing but give you more of the same, and they are not walking your path. **The moments that make you uncomfortable and even angry have the potential to truly change your life and make you grow.** All you need to do is unpack them and dig into what made you react. Alternatively, maybe it's about making a different choice and seeking something greater.

Discover the beliefs that play a major role in how you experience life. As the saying goes, if you believe you can, you will. If you believe you can't, you won't. Either way, you are correct. Your internal dialogue can be the undoing of the greatest idea. Self-doubt and negative thinking are the killers of forward movement. The moment of doubt that is left unchallenged can have long-term impacts in the direction and quality of your life, especially if it stops you acting.

When I had laser eye surgery, my mum offered to run me to and from the hospital and said she would ask for extra days off work. As I was on my own, I was grateful to have someone to care for me while my eyes were out of action. When push came to shove, she never asked for the time off. I raised this with her, letting her know how much it hurt. She responded that she had helped by looking after the girls for two weeks while I was still married, when my ex and I went on a holiday together, and that she couldn't be expected to do everything. Little did she consider that instance was over twelve months prior. I had no one else to rely on, and with my eyes out of action, I felt incredibly vulnerable. While working through this situation and others, I realised I believed I was an inconvenience to others. This impacted the way I interacted with people. Being overly grateful for small things and over-giving as a way of achieving acceptance. Doing this meant I gave less time to myself to achieve what I wanted, slowing my forward movement.

My relationship with my mum has been a rocky one. So many times, I forgave and accepted who she chose to be to maintain the relationship. With so many other moments of feeling shafted and hurt, I eventually reached breaking point. I wasn't prepared to hear any more of her excuses as to why it was okay to let me down. My expectations of those in my life are now higher than that. Part of believing a new story about yourself is changing your actions. Changing my belief that I was an inconvenience began with not accepting the behaviour that allowed me to think that I was.

Self-doubt and negative thinking are self-sabotage. You tell yourself that an idea won't be a success. That you shouldn't share the greatest achievements in your life because you don't want to stand out. I too doubt myself from time to time. I set visions and goals so high and beyond my wildest expectations that I don't even know how to get there. I just keep moving forward despite the uncertainty and fear. I find big dreams exhilarating, and I want to achieve them with every fibre of my being. I know there is something greater waiting for me. Ready to manifest. I can feel it. I just need to do the work to achieve it and never give up on me.

Fulfillment in life comes in many shades, and for everyone it looks different. There are many people who wish for nothing more than to work nine to five and be the best parent they can be. There is 100 percent nothing wrong with this dream. It is humble and incredibly beautiful. There are those with dreams as long as their arms who wonder if they will live long enough to achieve them. Then there is the mass of people who sit in the middle. Fearful of stepping outside of the norm for a variety of reasons. Fear stops way too many dreams from becoming reality and are often linked to beliefs.

I am one of the lucky ones. I have always had a sense that I was here to do something greater. To *be* something greater. The longer I have walked this path, the stronger that feeling has become. My willingness to put fear and uncertainty aside and continually rise has allowed me to blindly follow this gut feeling and listen to the quiet whispers from within.

There is one thing that has been proven again and again. The more I have grown and come to understand myself and the world around me, the better my life has become and the more joy I have been able to experience and share. When you begin to chase something with conviction and blind faith, things change and show up like they never have before. Guidance from your angels and other light beings seems to flow easily, and the people you need to meet seem to show up out of thin air. Life begins to become magical.

Magic is one of those things that's always available to you. You knew it as a kid. Through the process of "growing up", you began to lose sight of the magic. The good news is that you can reclaim the magic in your life. Doing so has been nothing short of miraculous for me in my life.

The ability to believe whole-heartedly in something that you have no real evidence of can be a challenge for the mind to grasp. Every logical part of your brain just wants to see or experience the evidence using all the senses. Call me crazy but when I hear stories of people who are in places such as the Irish countryside, or other places where there are ancient woods, and they share stories of fairies, I love to believe them. How beautiful is the possibility of a world filled with magic, and how dull is a world void of it?

Magic occurs in life every single day. It may not be fairies or anything comfortable, but it is a gift in the end. Maybe you have begun to see repetitive numbers on the clock, or on car number plates. Often, we start by seeing '11:11'. These numbers are a way in which your guides are communicating with you, trying to get your attention. If you start to see them, thank your guides for their guidance and look up what those numbers mean. I remember when I first started to see them. I was a few years into my personal development journey. I would see the same numbers everywhere and for days on end. Acknowledging them only enough to say, 'Oh wow, I saw those numbers the other day too. How strange.'

At the same time, there would be situations or people in my life that I would be struggling with. Eventually, I twigged these numbers might have a greater meaning and started looking them up. Initially, I would look them up once the drama had died down. I would always roll my eyes and *tut-tut* myself, because the information that would have helped me get through whatever was going on in my life at those times was contained in the meanings of those numbers. So, if you start seeing them, look them up. They are there to guide you and help you. It's why I incorporated them into the book.

In a world where tomorrow is never guaranteed, what will you choose to believe, see, strive for, and achieve? There is so much more available to you than you may imagine. You cannot want something more for another than for yourself, because it defeats the purpose. There must first be the willingness to have and achieve it for yourself. To experience the joy available, you must first be willing to find that joy within yourself. **To have the success you truly desire, you must be willing to make the unpopular choices to make it happen.**

This book has been written over different times of the day and night, waking at silly hours not being able to sleep and with a new idea that I wanted to share. It's easier and more comfortable to say, 'Hey I'll do it later.' Later doesn't seem to come. I can't even begin to express the number of great ideas I have lost because I didn't write them down or put them into some form of action at the time because I told myself I would act on it in the morning. Then ending up unable to recall what it was. Often, those nuggets of wisdom never returned.

At every moment of every day, we are faced with choices. What to eat, what to wear, what to say, and what to do. We also have the choice as to whether we will take that next breath. Right now, you could choose to hold your breath for as long as you can. You would continue to experience the discomfort until you choose to take another breath. **Choices will drive your life. The small choices you make everyday matter as they accumulate over time.** So, what will your next choice be and in what direction will it be taking you?

29 - Final Note

Here we have arrived at the final chapter, and I feel lost for words. With having said so much already, there is still an amazing journey ahead. It's hard to find which words to say. I guess my heart would first like to say thank you for picking up this book and being curious enough to read it through. I can only trust that its pages held something beautiful for you to discover.

It's highly possible you have already transformed and learnt things through the process of reading this book. The most important thing I want you to realise is that this incredible gift called life is ultimately about you rediscovering who you are and not taking life for granted. It's unravelling all the things you are told you "should" be and forgiving yourself and others. Reach the point where you can say you live with peace in your heart and mind.

This journey is not about being perfect. It's the complete opposite. It's messy, doesn't follow a logical path, and zigs when you zag. You are going to mess up many times, and as much as I have tried to spare you the effort of some of the learning, you will have your own specific lessons to learn. It is about aiming to be one percent better every day and ensuring you find a reason to get up, get dressed, and make your bed first thing in the morning. **Making small positive changes every day will change your life. You deserve so much happiness.**

Learn to trust in you and your intuition. It will guide you through even the darkest of tunnels and often in mysterious directions. These intuitive nudges will be your guides helping to light the way. Follow them. They take you where you need to go, even when that's towards a new lesson. Just know that whatever life and your guides throw at you, you can trust in yourself. The more you believe in you, the higher you will climb, no matter the mountain. Life is never going to go the way you think. It will get a shake-up from time to time, and this is a good thing. The more challenges you face, the more you will grow. With experience it gets easier. Nothing in life is stagnant. It will always change, move and evolve. Be willing to grow. The universe will force your hand if you resist. I believe this is what happened in my marriage breakdown. Had that not happened, I may never have finished this book. Walking down that lonely road gave me the insight that I was not the only one struggling, and I needed to get back on the keyboard to help even one more person.

If you expect life to change, you will find yourself better equipped to recognise and accept the change. The person who adapts that fastest will be the greatest success. The adaptability of the human species puts us at the top of the food chain. Life is ever changing. The quicker you adapt, the faster you will grow.

When I look out into the sea of faces that pass me every day, I am reminded why I do this. It's the lady who is smiling, though it doesn't reach her eyes. The person accepting the status quo because they believe that is all life has to offer. It's the man in the suit who is so rigid as he walks because he is trying to be what is expected of him, rather than what his soul would love him to be. It's the child who is wild and full of life who reminds me where we come from. It's the friend who still wears the mask to hide the pain of the stories she tells herself in private. I watch each of these beautiful souls walk by, unaware of the joy not so far away. I give them my most genuine smile, hoping to brighten their day just a little and be the space of light, love, and possibility.

There are still days that I am grumpy and sad. I embrace those days too. It might just mean I need to incorporate more self-love into my day and courageously step forward into what's challenging me. During the times when I am feeling whole, I stare out my window and breathe in the peace of the moment. Enjoying the trees in the beautiful afternoon light. Acknowledging with gratitude the contribution they make to my life and everyone else's.

Gratitude will change your life, as will learning to become vulnerable. Stepping into your authenticity will allow you to explore and discover who you are. This life you are living right now is a gift. No matter what is going on for you, each bad day has a silver lining, and every lesson learnt has a purpose. Nothing is by accident. It's all taking you in the direction of the road you are destined to travel. As much as roads twist and turn, go up and down and offer options to go left or right, all these roads lead back to you. Who you truly are at the core of your heart and soul is where the roads are headed. I am so excited that you—even just by reading this book—are exploring the possibility of accessing the happiness and peace that is truly possible.

I can only trust that my story and what I have learnt over my years of growth will find a place in your heart and allow you to uncover greater possibilities in your life. Either through healing a past hurt, finding greater meaning in the simple things, or gaining access to even more of your authentic self. I hope you harness the courage and strength I cultivated through the darkest times in my life and find the light in your life. No matter what has happened, it wasn't meant to be the end. Maybe just a new beginning. A new possibility to create something different.

The road you choose will always be yours. **Know that anything that is truly meant for you will not pass you by.** I take comfort in this on the days it takes all the faith I can muster to put one foot in front of the other. People will come and go, and situations will occur to allow something greater to enter your life. Make space for it. Have faith no matter what. Something wonderful will happen.

In the end, finding the courage to heal and grow is about discovering yourself and embracing the magic of life. Enjoying the cool breeze on a warm summer night. Learning to love yourself more than you love others. You can only meet others at the depth that you meet yourself. The love you find for yourself is filled with compassion, kindness, and understanding. There is no judgement, only acceptance. You may not be happy with your body, job, finances, or some other area of life right now, but you are perfectly positioned on your journey. You are perfect in this very moment. You are where you're meant to be. If you were meant to be somewhere else, that is where you would be. Life would make sure of that. You've got this, and you are never alone.

- ∞ Go within and find you. The one you've been hiding, who you've been thinking wasn't good enough.
- ∞ Go find you. The one who has hidden hopes and dreams and is willing to chase them.
- ∞ Go find you. The one with the big heart who is willing to become the light and hope.
- ∞ Go find your joy, peace and love. Live it, be it, embrace it.

The quality of your life is up to you and the daily choices you make.

Are you ready?

Thank you for taking the time to read *Walk with Me*. Your journey is just beginning, and I would love to hear your thoughts on this book and the parts you found most valuable. May each of your days be filled with joy and possibilities beyond your wildest imagination.

Kylee

About

Kylee Van Der Vuurst was guided into the world of healing and personal development by twists of fate and faith in herself, and a greater vision.

A mother to two incredible young women, a qualified life coach, energy healer, nutritionist and Pilates instructor, she has not only improved her life and the life of those around her but the life of the many who have utilised her services.

This knowledge base provides a unique perspective to holistic growth and healing.

Combined with her life experience, she has created this incredible story of growth through hardship and learning.

This is just the beginning for this dedicated woman as she aims to build on her ripple effect to positively change people's lives each and every day.

For Further Information

Amy Cuddy's TED Talk on body language:

https://youtu.be/2ToU6tIQDnA

Joanne Walmsley – Sacred Scribes - Angel Numbers –

https://sacredscribes.blogspot.com/p/angel-numbers.html

www.ingramcontent.com/pod-product-compliance
Lightning Source LLC
Chambersburg PA
CBHW022220090526
44585CB00013BB/591